For Marianna
with love

Walking
Long Street

Desmond Martin

Desmond Martin

page 33

Desmond Martin

page 46

An illustrated walk up Cape Town's best-loved street with architectural and historical commentary and personal anecdotes from the 1950s

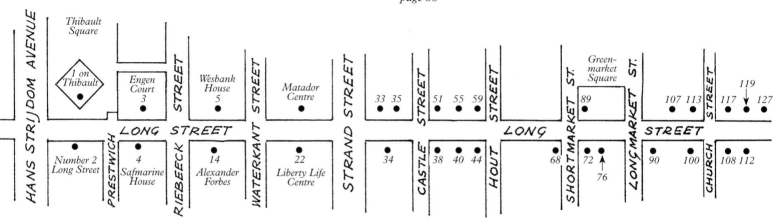

page 95

page 65

Walking
Long Street

Text and watercolours by **Desmond Martin**

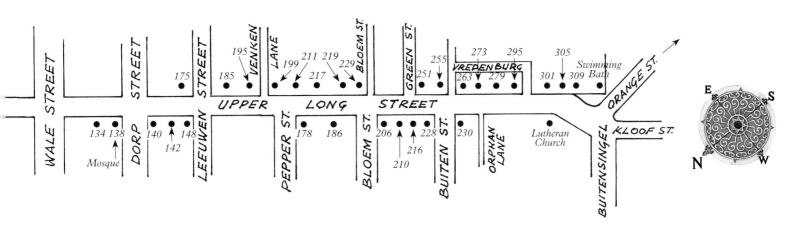

Published by Struik Publishers (a division of
New Holland Publishing (South Africa) (Pty) Ltd)
New Holland Publishing is a member of Johnnic Communications Ltd
Cornelis Struik House, 80 McKenzie Street, Cape Town 8001
86 Edgware Road, London, W2 2EA, United Kingdom
Unit 1, 66 Gibbes Street, Chatswood, NSW 2067, Australia
218 Lake Road, Northcote, Auckland, New Zealand

www.struik.co.za

Publishing manager: Linda de Villiers
Editor: Cecilia Barfield
Architectural editor: John Rennie
Designer: Helen Henn
Illustrator: Desmond Martin
Proofreader: Irma van Wyk

Reproduction: Hirt & Carter Cape (Pty) Ltd
Printing and binding: Craft Print International
Ltd, Singapore

ISBN 978-1-77007-508-5

10 9 8 7 6 5 4 3 2 1

Over 40 000 unique African images available to purchase
from our image bank at **www.imagesofafrica.co.za**

Acknowledgements

Producing this tribute to Long Street has been made all the more enjoyable by a number of very special people:

Firstly, it was Marianna, my wife, who encouraged me to illustrate and write about Long Street when I was vacillating between a couple of subjects for a book. Having settled on my year at the YMCA as the springboard for my project, I contacted Stan Fish to corroborate what I had written about our former 'home'. I appreciate his involvement and for providing the 1950s photograph of YM lads in the Cape Town Gardens. In similar vein, historical facts of the YWCA were kindly sent to me by Marion Pallant. For information on conservation legislation currently applicable to Long Street, I am grateful to Jim Hallinan of the Heritage Resources Section, City of Cape Town.

I am especially indebted to Cape Town architect John Rennie for his role as architectural editor. The comprehensive building survey of Central Cape Town that he undertook on behalf of the former Cape Provincial Institute of Architects (CPIA) nearly 30 years ago provided me with architectural information of Long Street's buildings as they were in 1978. Together with my own observations and recollections, *Walking Long Street* began to take shape. John subsequently identified a number of architects not named in his survey and supplied additional technical and historical data for certain buildings for which I am grateful. His comments on the opinions I have expressed were invaluable.

To the loosely knit Long Street community – café and restaurant managers, property owners, tenants and others – thank you for the snippets of information that injected additional spice into my Long Street tale. Finally, to the publishing team at Struik I record my appreciation for their co-operation and positive criticism of my literary and illustrative work.

Deo Gratias.

Contents

I lived in Long Street

In mid-year 1954, as a young lad of seventeen, I moved into my first home-from-home, the Young Men's Christian Association (YMCA) at 44 Long Street (see illustration opposite). In the year that followed I began a love affair with the buildings around my new home, a fascination that has been an unbroken romance for half a century. Thus Long Street became *my* Long Street.

Fifty years on the time had arrived to document in word and watercolour the story of the street's older buildings and, with the YMCA as the nodal point, to record selected incidents from my youth while living at that illustrious address, the stage on which these stories were played out. If by illustration and anecdote the conservation of Long Street can be enhanced, my time will have been well spent.

Instead of terming this an introduction, I prefer to call it a pre-amble as it begs to be read before any visit or walk is attempted in Long Street. The emphasis is on 'amble', which means to move at an easy pace. When you examine the old buildings, scan the merchandise in the shop windows or simply enjoy the ambiance of a street of a bygone era – you dare not rush. For the lovers of architectural styles that pre-date the coming of the modern concrete-framed office blocks (that differ little from one city to the next), there is an amazing variety of buildings to view, each with its very own frivolous and often meaningless ornamentations. But all of them ask to be remembered and make mute appeals to be photographed so that, should you have come to Cape Town from a distant town or land, you will have a pleasurable record of your amble in Long Street. I have therefore included a few practical walking tips at the end of this pre-amble that could ensure that your day is both memorable and trouble free. And for those who dabble with watercolours I have also added some explanatory comments about my illustrations.

In more serious vein, in the following section I have attempted to explain how Long Street has managed to survive the demolitions that accompanied the accelerated property development in Cape Town since the 1950s. My overview pays tribute to the remarkable efforts made by various individuals and organizations to protect and conserve Long Street as a valuable grouping of historical buildings.

Anecdotes from the 1950s

Thankfully, the Long Street I knew 50 years ago is not too different from the Long Street that thousands of visitors to Cape Town can still see and enjoy today. Though numerous attractions of the thoroughfare are now tourism related, the old buildings, many sporting brightly coloured façades, look more charming than when I first saw them in 1954, the year that my brother and I left our family home in a Cape Town suburb to take up residence in the city.

At the YMCA we were allocated a smallish room, Number 42, on the third floor, directly above the side entrance in Hout Street. I was soon to discover the strategic importance of that room as it played

SERVICE
REPAIRS GO

Desmond Martin

Right: *Hout Street façade of the old YMCA with the Oak Hall on the left. Room 42 is on the top floor in the middle*

Desmond Martin

a prominent role in the YMCA's unofficial 'ceremony of the keys'. England boasts of its Ceremony of the Keys at the Tower of London and Cape Town can be proud of its own key ceremony performed at the Castle. Our ritual at the YMCA was never performed for an audience, neither did any of the residents know when a 'ceremony' would start – but we were always ready to participate with the enthusiasm and brashness of youth.

It worked in the following manner. All of the 25 residents were issued keys for the side door along with their room keys. There was no curfew imposed on the young men and we were free to return 'home' at any hour. The privilege was seldom abused but occasionally someone would return home from a night out at an unacceptable hour without his side door keys. Standing in Hout Street, well back from the door, he would shout loudly to the darkened windows on the second and third floors above, 'Keys, keys!'

On being awakened, the sleeping residents responded by reaching out for containers of water and, like programmed soldiers, awaited the next move. The call would be made again, 'Keys, keys.' One of the residents would then throw his own keys into the street, carefully aiming for the bunch to land on the tarmac about two metres in front of the building below his window. As the latecomer dashed to retrieve the keys he had to dodge the cascade of water released by the residents above. He would then rush for the door, but even at the entrance he was not safe because the door opens outwards. If my brother and I were quick enough we were able to fire another direct watery salvo from the ramparts. And so would end the ceremony of the keys. There was no applause from spectators – maybe just a few muffled chuckles as residents went back to bed and a dampened resident stomped loudly up the wooden staircase to his room.

The YMCA building, now known under another name, is still there for all to see, though it was in danger of demolition in 1978. My third floor room and the side entrance are both unchanged. I invite you during your Long Street walk to turn the corner into Hout Street and look up at the building at the point shown in my watercolour. Perhaps if you are brazen enough to ignore the stares of passers-by, you will even be moved to shout aloud, 'KEYS' and in your mind's eye see the re-enactment of the old YMCA keys ceremony.

Another incident comes to mind that, to my knowledge, fortunately only happened twice. If you look at the watercolour of the YMCA opposite, you will notice the wide projecting bracketed cornice (ledge) just below the third floor windows. The building was originally only three storeys high before the top floor was added. This main cornice had been at roof parapet level and thus stood out a good deal more than the moulding between the first and second floors.

One night, my brother Peter became involved in a water fight with residents in the passage on the top floor. After a few watery exchanges he retreated to his bedroom and locked the door. Climbing through his window onto the ledge three floors above street level and armed with two water jugs, he stealthily made his way along the ledge until he reached the open windows of his fellow residents on the Hout Street side. Imagine their surprise when they were dowsed with water coming from this unexpected direction! My sure-footed brother retreated the way he had come and was safe in his room before his victims had dried themselves off. I thought my brother had pioneered the 'ledge walk', but according to a YMCA resident of earlier vintage, another sure-footed boarder with the nickname of 'Ox' had been the first to 'walk the ledge' prior to 1955. These stories, now largely forgotten even by YM old boys, deserve to be recorded in print for their daring.

Possibly in earlier days at the height of the fervour for Queen and Empire (c.1900), the two flagpoles on the verandah of the YMCA sported Union Jacks. Shortly before my brother and I took up residence in 1954, one of the flagpoles featured in yet another prank. Apparently annoyed by the constant presence of a rusty old bicycle parked on the verandah, a resident fastened the two wheels of the bike to the rope and ran the bicycle up the pole like a flag. There it flapped for some while until angry boarders from the hotel across the street, the Langham Hotel (see page 38), reported the lark to the YMCA office.

The building was designated in two places as the YMCA by large red, cast-iron letters fixed to the verandah railings. One of the tamer tricks that was repeated from time-to-time was to invert the two 'M' letters to read 'YWCA', possibly in the hope that some damsel would climb the staircase and enquire about lodging. Though I indulged in this letter-inverting custom and closely watched its effects on the passing parade, not a single young lady was ever misled. In later years one or two more adventurous YM lads applied the 'letter-inverting' prank in reverse on the YWCA building – No. 78 Long Street. Under cover of darkness they scaled its verandah and turned the 'W' upside-down to read 'YMCA'. The local matron was not amused.

A decided drawback to living in the city was the distance from the beaches. Sun-loving residents determined to acquire healthy suntans could walk down Long Street to catch the bus to Sea Point if time was not an issue. YM residents, ever alive to shortcuts and innovation, had found a popular alternative to the long bus ride in search of the sun. Adjoining the YM building is a two-storey shop, No. 42, currently Gordon's Hardware. It has a corrugated-iron roof, hidden from the street by a parapet wall. By climbing through the only window on the YMCA's wall overlooking the shop, residents could access the hot tin roof and enjoy the sun in complete privacy. When the time came to cool off, the showers in the YM's gymnasium were close at hand.

YM residents in my time were largely church-going, which is no surprise considering that the 'CA' stood for 'Christian Association'. As was the custom in the 1950s, 'Sunday observance' was not regarded as restrictive and, after a hearty breakfast on Sunday mornings, residents walked with purpose to places of worship in the city, some to the Groote Kerk in Adderley Street, some to the Metropolitan Methodist Church on Greenmarket Square, a few to the Cape Town Baptist Church in Wale Street (near the corner of Long Street) and others elsewhere.

After the service it was the custom of the YM lads to walk to the tearoom in the Company Gardens at the top of Adderley Street and enjoy a milkshake or ginger beer. The photograph from the early 1950s shows six of the residents, dressed in their double-breasted baggy suits, posing in the sun near the tearoom.

As evidenced by the photograph, 'Sunday dress' had to be your best. If you had a suit, you wore it. And with it you wore a tie even if the weather was stinking hot. This led me, in the summer of 1955, to indulge in an innovative fashion change.

I maintained that bow ties were cooler than the common necktie and persuaded a church-going friend to adopt the bow tie for Sunday. In addition, to keep the sun from our faces while walking to church, we bought straw boaters, or as they were then known, 'cheese cutters'. It was an accepted headgear at some Cape Town boys' schools so I did not think it was too avant-garde for the YMCA. Sporting cheese cutters and red triangle YM badges on our hatbands, bow ties, white shirts and our old grey school suits with their exceptionally baggy trousers, we set off up Long Street for church one Sunday, much to the embarrassment of the more staid YM residents. The photograph shows me (on the right) with friend Charles Smith on the roof of the YMCA after attending church. Other residents declined to adopt the modified dress and to my great disappointment, the fashion died with my departure from the YM later in the year.

The YWCA, as the sister organization to the YMCA, was quite naturally a well-known building to the lads from No. 44. As one would have expected, access to the YW building was carefully guarded. I remember in my year at the YMCA that at regular intervals the invitation would be

Top: *A group of YMCA residents from the 1950s*
Bottom: *Charles Smith (left) with the author (1955)*

received from the matron of the YWCA to have tea with the girls after church on a Sunday evening. Still in our baggy Sunday attire, about ten young men would walk into the YW at the appointed time, climb the stairs to the reception room on the first floor and engage in stilted conversation with about twice as many ladies, all dressed in their prettiest but modest attire. It was then that I had the rare privilege of standing on the first floor Victorian verandah and seeing what *my* Long Street looked like from this female preserve. All too soon the tea party would end and the YM lads would be escorted to the front door. Despite the matron's tight control of proceedings, a few romances did bloom and some even culminated in wedding bells.

Living at the 'Y' in the 1950s was carefree and we saw little of crime on the streets. Though the majority of the residents had to be frugal with their small salaries, many happily gave freely of their time and energy to the various YMCA activities. There was also an awareness of the low-income communities close by. Some residents joined with other YM members, giving tuition and assisting with physical training and recreation at the Boys' Club run by the YMCA in a hired building in Chiappini Street, five blocks up from Long Street. Others served as Sunday School teachers in the poorer neighbourhoods of Cape Town. My commitment was to the tiny Jarvis Street Baptist Church in Green Point, now being used as an art gallery. But as young men we were blissfully unaware of the threats to Cape Town's old architecture such as road widening plans, large-scale development of city blocks and the more subtle menace of urban decay. Neither were we aware of the evils of forced removals that would overtake entire communities on the eastern side of town in District Six during the next decade. So for the happy memories of my Long Street that cannot be erased, I am thankful.

Walking Long Street – a few tips

If I should contemplate a walk to see the street's architectural charms, where would I begin?

Do I walk up towards Table Mountain? Or should I start at the top and walk down towards the sea? The answer is that it doesn't really matter, but as I have catalogued the entries in numerical order, it would be logical to walk up the street. To save yourself from frequent crossings of the street to see buildings on the opposite side, I suggest you walk up one side and down the other. Which side to choose will depend on the season, the weather and how much shade or sun you prefer. Remember the African sun is fierce; always wear a hat and use plenty of sun block otherwise by nightfall you will regret that you even heard of Long Street.

Another factor to bear in mind is that Long Street is a one-way street with the traffic moving up from the sea towards Table Mountain.

If you have travelled into the city by car I suggest you find safe legal parking somewhere on the foreshore or at the parking garage on Thibault Square. Most of the late twentieth century buildings are built in lower Long Street, between Hans Strijdom Avenue and Strand Street, so to appreciate the stark contrast of styles between these towering office blocks and the Victorian, Edwardian and Art Deco styles of the buildings in the upper parts of Long Street, I suggest that you begin your walk in the shadow of an impressive 30-storey tower, 'No. 1 Thibault Square'. If the international style of the high-rise buildings holds little interest for you, you could ignore them and make a start at No. 33, the first 'old' building just beyond the Strand Street intersection. Look for the inscription on the parapet, 'H.C. Collison Ltd. 1815'.

Set aside three hours for 'walking' Long Street – one hour for walking up, an hour for lunch and another hour's walk back to your car. The more time you have to look, the more you will enjoy the walk.

Identifying the buildings: In the following sections of text I have identified buildings by their street numbers as these have remained largely unchanged for the last 40 or so years. In addition to the number, I have used the name of the building where it appears somewhere on the building itself or if it is generally known by that name, for example, 'the Blue Lodge', pictured below. In many cases where a building is not named, I have resorted to using the name of the current tenant or owner, as it is the signage you are likely to see when walking. Unfortunately this is not the best option, as businesses do close and new businesses open from time to time. The watercolour in conjunction with the street number is therefore your best guide to identifying buildings.

Desmond Martin

Photography: You will not need to be reminded that buildings do not photograph well around midday, as shadows are minimal. Early morning or late afternoon photos generally produce better shots. Late afternoon shadows in Long Street, especially in the winter months, tend to creep across the street very quickly and can block out the lower section of buildings. Take your photos while you can unless you have time to return another day.

Safety: Take the usual precautions when walking in the city. Walking with someone is also more fun and safer than walking alone.

About the watercolours

I have purposely included as much detail of the buildings in Long Street as the eye can accommodate, though it is a well-accepted fact in the art world that too much detail in a painting leaves the beholder 'unemployed'. The viewer is usually allowed and encouraged to imagine some aspects of the picture not finalized by the artist. My focus, however, is to record for posterity the architectural gems of Long Street as I saw them in 2005 and as my camera captured them on film. Years ago I chose to sketch my architectural subjects in a fine sepia line before applying colour washes. I found that demarcating areas by line work was more suitable for this type of illustration than the usual pencil-guided washes that watercolourists use. Although minute details are obviously omitted on account of the small scale of my artwork, I aimed at producing a faithful record of the architect's design and the builders' achievements rather than my own idealistic interpretation of the subject.

Clouds play an important role in most of the watercolours. By their very fluidity, they introduce an element of freedom to the picture that is otherwise dominated by straight lines of the architectural shapes. Clouds are still the most exciting natural phenomena to depict, as they are constantly on the move, changing shape as one watches. Three-dimensional buildings must obey the rules of perspective whereas clouds often defy all these rules, riding across the picture oblivious of pictorial conventions.

So much of the delight of watercolour paintings relies on the preservation of selected white areas. These I have sought to achieve by using art masking fluid rather than recovering highlights with Chinese white. The human figures and motor vehicles in the illustrations have been left only partially painted so as not to compete with the buildings that need to take centre stage. These nameless people and cars could have been omitted, but without them the picture would suggest a scene from a sterile film set. The figures also give scale and life to the illustration, reminding the viewer that without them in real life, Long Street would indeed crumble into ruins.

I hope that my watercolours will remind you of busy, colourful, exciting, lively Long Street every time you scan through this book.

Desmond Martin
Cape Town
December 2006

How has Long Street survived?

Why is it that so much of 'olde worlde' Long Street survives? How has Cape Town been able to retain a significant mass of the old building fabric of Long Street despite the march of progress into the twenty-first century? Part of the credit is undoubtedly attributable to the combined efforts of the Cape Town City Council, the National Monuments Council (NMC) (name subsequently changed in 2000), concerned architects and planners within the then Cape Provincial Institute of Architects (CPIA) and at the University of Cape Town, as well as support from organizations such as the Vernacular Architecture Society, the Simon van der Stel Foundation, the Cape Town Heritage Trust and the local media.

Aside from these groups, it may be that the average Capetonian is subconsciously aware of the culture of conservation in the city. An appreciation for the history of the 'Tavern of the Seas', as Cape Town has been called, and the various cultures that have left their imprint on its old buildings has slowly taken root. How or when this awareness began is impossible to pinpoint. As early as 1888 Mrs Koopmans de Wet, an ardent protagonist for conservation, intervened successfully against the Imperial government's plans to demolish Cape Town's Castle of Good Hope. In 1896, when the road skirting the Castle was to be widened for the new electric trams, she withstood demands from Prime Minister Cecil Rhodes to cut off one of the Castle's famous bastions. In the 100 years since, there have been countless incidents when individuals, academic institutions and heritage organizations have acted in various ways with the Cape Town City Council to control development in the City and save buildings and other historical structures from being destroyed or radically altered.

I recall that in the 1970s and early 1980s, the fashion for restoring old furniture, in particular the cottage furniture of the 1920s and 1930s became fairly widespread, with a preference for solid wood items especially if made of Oregon pine. Restoration did not stop with furniture and complete houses were renovated and restored to how they were when first built. Wherever these restored buildings were also correctly maintained, it could be said that conservation was being applied. Outside the inner city in the older parts of Cape Town, where Victorian cottages were still intact, these became highly desirable. In 1981, over 20 houses in Wynberg's 'Chelsea Village' to the south of Carr Hill were proclaimed national monuments to ensure controlled restoration. In the years that followed scores of houses and buildings in other suburbs were similarly declared. A conservation ethic slowly permeated the community of Cape Town as the pace quickened to recycle old homes and buildings.

Desmond Martin

Above: *Part of No. 148, restored in 1982*

Above: *No. 40,*
SA Slave Church
(Museum)

It was in the late 1970s that a road-widening plan for Hout and Shortmarket Streets was proposed. This controversial plan threatened to destroy many historical buildings in the central city, not only in the two named streets but also in Long Street where notably the YMCA would have been demolished. Fortunately, the City authorities abandoned the plan in 1978, but it served as a warning to all of the vulnerability of Cape Town's vintage architecture.

During the decade of the 1970s, only 34 properties in the entire Cape Peninsula were declared 'monuments' by the NMC. In the next 15 years between 1980 and 1995, the pressure to protect historical properties, mainly houses, in Cape Town and the Peninsula, increased dramatically and 232 proclamations of 'monuments' appeared in the *Government Gazette*. Among these were eight fine buildings in Long Street proclaimed between 1977 and 1993, namely the South African Missionary Society (SA Slave Church (Museum)) (No. 40), the Blue Lodge hotel (No. 208), the YWCA (No. 78/80), the Home of Arthur Elliott (No. 134), Tyne Buildings (No. 140), Dorfman & Katz Building (No. 142), Wiener Bakery (No. 148) and the YMCA (No. 44). These particular proclamations not only protected the buildings from demolition, but also demonstrated to the public-at-large that steps were being taken to save historical structures in Long Street. The Blue Lodge hotel, restored to its former splendour in 1982 by the owner in collaboration with his architects, set the standard for the many restorations in Long Street that were to follow.

In 1990, the restoration of Winchester House (No. 72/74/76 Long Street) generated much controversy among conservationists when the two façades, one on Long Street and the other on Shortmarket Street, were secured by scaffolding to allow the balance of the building to be gutted and rebuilt, a version of conservation known as 'facadism'. Most conservationists hold the view that retaining only the façade of a building ignores all that is historical and significant within. Unfortunately, if a business cannot function efficiently within an old interior then facadism is the compromise between two options – maintainence of a dated, useless building **or** the total demolition of the building so that it may be rebuilt to modern standards. Facadism has been successfully used elsewhere in Cape Town and in 2005 two delightful buildings in Hout Street were spared total demolition and their façades retained in 'The Decks' building project at the corner of Long and Hout Streets.

Before 1978, conservation bodies such as the NMC and City Council lacked detailed historical and architectural information on which to base their decisions to formally protect old buildings in Cape Town. In the face of the increasing pace of property development and under the leadership of architect Revel Fox, the

CPIA took positive action in 1977 to survey the historical fabric in Cape Town's central business district. John Rennie was appointed to undertake the mammoth task of inspecting and documenting relevant details of over 900 buildings 'of all shapes and sizes … spread among the oldest colonial streets and civic spaces in the Republic'. At the end of 1978, Volumes 1 and 2 of *The Buildings of Central Cape Town* were published by the CPIA. These volumes, together with Volume 3 compiled in 1985 by a team of three architects, represent the most comprehensive inventory of Cape Town's buildings at that time. Volume 2 contains 100 photographs with accompanying text on buildings in Long Street.

Two other commentaries that provide invaluable information on the Cape's historic buildings were also published at this time, these being Désirée Picton-Seymour's *Victorian Buildings in South Africa* (Balkema, 1977) and *The Old Buildings of the Cape* (Balkema, 1980) by Hans Fransen and Mary Cook. Both books include numerous references to Long Street buildings.

Though the NMC worked hand-in-hand with the City Council in protecting individual historical properties, the backlog of buildings deserving protection did not appear to decrease! After a decade of attempts to resolve the problem, the Cape Town City Council in 1990 introduced a far-reaching amendment to the 1985 Land Use Planning Ordinance (LUPO), namely the introduction of Urban Conservation Areas. In short, this allowed extensive urban areas to be declared so that blanket protection could be given to all the properties in a designated area.

Simultaneous with the passing of the 1990 LUPO amendment, five renowned public squares in Cape Town, the Lutheran Church complex in Strand Street and Wynberg Village were proclaimed conservation areas. Recognition of Long Street's architectural and historical credentials was formalized in 1992 when Upper Long Street was designated as an urban conservation area along with two areas in the Upper Table Valley. Late in 1994, the locality in the Long Street Study along with twelve other urban conservation areas was consolidated into the greater Central City Urban Conservation Area, the status of which was approved by the Cape Provincial Administration in 1997.

All buildings in Long Street thus enjoy the protection given to buildings and structures in urban conservation areas and, in theory, are safe from unauthorized demolition. Consent to demolish or alter individual properties within the area can be denied if it is thought that proposed changes 'will be detrimental to the protection and/or historical significance' of the area. As most of the older buildings of Long Street are more than 60 years old, they are additionally protected as 'historical artefacts' by the National Heritage Resources Act No. 25 of 1999. The City's Heritage Resources Section closely monitors development in Long Street as well as the 28 other Urban Conservation Areas that have been established. These currently extend from Sea Point to the city centre and down the peninsula as far as Simon's Town.

A comparison of the Long Street buildings in *The Buildings of Central Cape Town* and the structures that can still be seen today shows how little the street has changed and how few of the buildings have been lost, a worthy tribute to all who have sought over a number of decades to conserve Long Street as an architectural showcase.

Right: *Engen Court
(left), Safmarine
House (centre) and
'No. 1 on Thibault'
from Thibault Square*

Desmond Martin

The buildings of
Long Street
below Strand

Eight massive high-rise buildings stand on either side of Long Street on the long upward slope between Hans Strijdom Avenue, on the edge of the Foreshore and Strand Street. As you move up the street between these concrete-framed office blocks with their smooth marble and terrazzo facings, you could sense a feeling of insignificance, especially if you stop for a moment and look upwards. The buildings rise up as stark unassailable ramparts, they hem you in and the virtual absence of doors on street level send an intimidating message that, if you have no business to do in the central business district, you are not too welcome there.

This is not a new criticism of architecture of the latter half of the twentieth century, for I have heard architects voice these concerns before. Further up Long Street, among the two-, three- and four-storey Victorian edifices, many with first floor verandahs, one is more aware of their human scale and how this characteristic contributes to making people feel at ease. All eight of the buildings at the lower end of Long Street were erected in the decades after my year at the YMCA and thus were never part of *my* Long Street. Their significance to me is that before they could rise up, something had to come down. Expansion and growth does have a price and in Long Street, as is the case in other historic parts of Cape Town, that price is invariably some loss of our architectural heritage.

With my illustrative focus on the older and more historic structures higher up the street, my comments on the buildings at the lower end are understandably brief. But to totally ignore their presence would be unfair to the creative spirit and skills of contemporary architects, engineers and building managers in our construction industry who have kept pace with the enormous technological advances in the building world. Each of the buildings named below is a version of the international architectural style, an approach devoid of national character so that similar designs may be seen in most modern cities of the world. They are thus representative of the significant expansion and development in the Mother City in the decades after 1960.

I have vague memories from the 1950s and later years of some of the old buildings that made way for the new, hence the nostalgic references and illustrations that are interwoven with my brief descriptions of the eight existing structures. This nostalgia of mine seeks not to belittle the present; rather, it urges me to memorialize architectural gems of the past.

No. 1 Long Street
'No. 1 on Thibault' (formerly BP Centre)

Set at an angle of 45° to Long Street and bordering on Thibault Square, this striking near 30-storey tower block completed in 1973 makes a worthy contribution to Cape Town's skyline. Horizontal bands of windows and the charcoal grey exposed stone chip surfaces give the building an impression of great strength and durability. The architects, Revel Fox and Partners, were awarded the CPIA's Bronze Medal in 1973 for the design of this landmark building.

No. 2 Long Street
'Number 2 Long Street' (formerly Mobil House)

Erected in 1966, this building of some 23 storeys occupies the full block between Hans Strijdom Avenue and Prestwich Street. The ground floor is finished in black marble and beige ceramic tiles but the rows of windows in bronze aluminium create a rather monotonous grid on the upper floors. Recently added grid screens have transformed the bland parking levels just above the ground floor.

No. 3 Long Street
Engen Court

Clad in bands of gleaming cream and brown imported granite, Engen Court has its main entrance strategically placed on a corner facing Thibault Square. The façades on Long and Riebeeck Streets are without doors, shops or canopies and thus present a rather unfriendly exterior to passers by. The building comprises eight storeys and was constructed between 1984 and 1987 to a design by Louis Karol Architects.

No. 4 Long Street
Safmarine House

The most recent addition to lower Long Street, this 26-storey office block, magnificently finished on the ground floor in a greyish pink granite, is best viewed from Sea Street, a narrow roadway off Riebeeck Street that fronts the building. The impressive central tower soars up behind mature palm trees that partially screen the set-back concave entrance on Riebeeck Street. This view of the building makes the short detour from Long Street worthwhile. Safmarine House was completed in 1993 to a design by Louis Karol Architects.

Above: *Nineteenth century shops in lower Sea Street (demolished)*

Paging through an old drawing book of mine, I came across a hastily drawn sketch of lower Sea Street that I completed during a lunch hour in 1978. It shows five small Victorian buildings that, unbeknown to me, would be demolished to make way for Safmarine's skyscraper that demanded the sacrifice of many smaller buildings for its massive base. The ground floor of these backstreet, two-storey businesses, all built between 1899 and 1901, had already in the late 1970s been modernized with arched windows (illustrated above) and were probably of no great architectural merit. I have redrawn the original sketch as a reminder of what was once lower Sea Street, just a half block away from *my* Long Street of 1955.

No. 5 Long Street

Wesbank House

This unimposing concrete-framed block of between seven and eight storeys was built in 1971 to a design by Louis Karol Architects. Finished in a dirty pink, exposed aggregate, the five rows of upper windows dominate the façade while the rounded corners with their deep shaded recesses appear to brood over the street below. The intersection of Long and Waterkant Streets is an unhappy reminder to me that this was where St John's, an unusual stone Anglican church stood for over a century, diagonally facing the corner of the site (refer my watercolour below).

The church suffered the same fate as that of many inner city churches. As a town develops, congregations migrate to the suburbs. Decreased support from remaining members coupled with tempting offers from property developers is too much for a church governing body to resist. Sale and demolition of the church invariably follows. I visited St John's only twice in my YM days. There was a sense of peace within its walls. Alas, St John's is but a fading memory for a few old parishioners and other Capetonians as it was demolished in 1970. The incalculable loss of this unique stone building in the heart of Cape Town's CBD cannot be undone. It might have served as a restaurant, theatre, museum or simply a 'green lung' for frazzled business folk. How significant it would have been to declare St John's a protected heritage site – a spiritual house in the midst of all that is materialistic and transient in the financial hub of the city.

St John's was designed by the architect John Calvert and built between 1853 and 1857 by Peter Penketh who was responsible for designing and building St Martini, the Lutheran church at the top of Long Street. Penketh also designed four other churches in the city between 1848 and 1857 and was appointed Cape Town's City Engineer in 1858. Built in coursed rubble masonry, St John's comprised a five-bay central nave and side aisles with diagonal buttresses on the corners. The three-sided portico (entrance) was probably a later addition. The stone wall fronting the church sloped steeply down Waterkant Street.

Right: St John's Anglican Church (demolished), cnr of Long & Waterkant Streets

No. 14 Long Street
Alexander Forbes
This ten-storey office block is finished in a cream-coloured terrazzo cladding. Apart from the segmented arches in the canopy high over the Long Street pavement, the only features on the otherwise plain upper eight storeys are uninspiring horizontal bands of windows. Two very different buildings previously occupied this site. On the Riebeeck and Long Street corner stood the Kine Two cinema complex, formerly the Van Riebeeck Cinema built in about 1945. This building had a bold round corner entrance with vertical ribs of brown brick rising five storeys above the street. On the other corner facing Waterkant Street was Osborne House, better known as Garth Castle Bar, a quaint two-storey mid-Victorian building.

Corner of Long and Strand Streets
Matador Centre
Dating from 1973, this not unattractive 10-storey block designed by Ezra Greenblo is clad in cream-coloured precast panels. A flat cornice decorated with a simple fret separates the lower floors from the seven upper floors. Here the large square windows, each set within their own precast terrazzo frames, project slightly thereby creating an eye-catching pattern on the façade. The ground floor is of polished black granite and marble but unfortunately offers no sidewalk shade or shelter to pedestrians.

No. 22 Long Street
Liberty Life Centre ('22-on-Long')
This eight-storey building is finished in an attractive covering of multi-coloured, tiny stone chips. It was completed in the 1980s, replacing the Strand Apartments, formerly the historic White House Hotel that was built in 1893 to a design by John Parker. The White House, sporting its name in a large cast-iron sky sign on the roof, was a landmark in the 1950s and 1960s and I remember relaxing once on its iron two-storey verandah during my YM days. Inside the foyer it was all teak, glass and brass with an impressive central staircase. This grand old lady of Strand Street was demolished in June 1981.

Above: *The White House Hotel (demolished)*

H.S. COLLISON L?
1815

COLLISONS

Desmond
Martin

The buildings of
Long Street
between Strand and Wale

When you cross Strand Street from the lower part of Long Street, you are immediately in touch with the past. Ignore the 'modern' buildings on the corner that flank the street, the Strand Centre, built in 1967, on the left and on the right, the ten-storey Atkinson House that was built in the 1950s. Your journey begins when you caress the mosaic tiles in the threshold of Collison's Building on the left (No. 33) and the terracotta facings of the front of Gibson's Building on the right of the street (No. 34). These are building materials that have survived more than a hundred years, testimony to the workmanship of our forefathers. Let the pages that follow guide you all the way to the top of Long Street.

No. 33 and No. 35 Long Street *(on the left and right in illustration opposite)*
Collison's Building and Diembe Fula (Sene Diembe African Art
and Imocha Internet Café)

This tiny two-storey gem in my watercolour is dwarfed by the seven-storey concrete and brick Strand Centre on its left. Collison's nevertheless has the honour of being the first of the 60 or more 'old' buildings in the street. It carries the inscription on the parapet, 'H.C. Collison Ltd – 1815' but the date probably refers to the founding date of the company. The date of construction was somewhere nearer 1880.

Features to notice are the cast-iron columns supporting the canopy, the wrought-iron railings and the fine plastered cornice and parapet above the three flat-headed windows. It is suspected, however, that some of these were part of a twentieth century renovation. Worthwhile spotting at the entrance threshold is the Collison name in mosaic tiles.

To the right of Collison's Building, is a charming three-storey Victorian building (No. 35) that was probably built in the 1850s, though the verandah and elaborate plasterwork are thought to have been added in the 1890s. The upper cornice and small pediment supported by four pairs of consoles are particularly ornate. The architect obviously felt his building needed even more height and so added a high parapet above the cornice. Note the classical running scroll frieze immediately above the first floor windows that adds a Grecian touch to the design.

Desmond Martin

No. 34 Long Street

'T. Gibson & Co' (currently an art gallery and formerly Sellars Gents Outfitters)

Dwarfed by its neighbours on either side, this two-storey building is unique in that it is the only building on Long Street which is completely terracotta, a pinkish brown hard burnt-clay facing that was popular at the turn of the nineteenth century.

DKM

Gibson's has a particularly fine teak front door with a fanlight above (which is why I chose to illustrate the door) with a teak-framed shop window to the left, all set between decorated terracotta pilasters. These feature finely sculpted, open-mouthed human heads as capitals. The first floor, similarly treated in terracotta, comprises 'a large-pane arched show window … with various decorative details … columns, escutcheons, consoles and brackets' (Rennie survey). These escutcheons carry the monogram 'TG & Co' while the escutcheon in the middle of the wavy parapet bears the date '1896'. The keystone in the arched window on the first floor carries another sculpted head, but now missing from the upper wall are two large Medusa heads and the company's name in gilded letters. Also removed are the prominent squared pillars that stood at either end of the parapet. Based on the plans of a similar building in New York, Gibson's was designed by Anthony de Witt and erected in 1904 despite the earlier date on the pediment.

The gents outfitters, Sellars, operated in the building for many years and during my working days in the city, I purchased at least two of my office suits at bargain prices at No. 34. I have vivid memories of long racks of gentlemen's suits and sports jackets on both floors of the shop that reawaken in my nostrils the agreeable smell of clean woven cloth.

Above:
Façade of No. 34
Opposite:
Entrance detail of No. 34

Desmond Martin

No. 38 Long Street *(cnr of Castle Street)*
Hotel Metropole

Although this hotel has been refurbished and altered a number of times in more than a century, the basic design remains much as it was when it opened in 1895 as Hotel Metropole (though the original 1894 plans named the building as the 'Hamburg Hotel'). A newspaper report in *The Cape Argus*, 1 July 1895, stated that it was 'one of the landmarks of the city … five storeys high … a tower at the corner rising over 90 feet above the street level. It is of a very imposing and grand appearance, being designed in the old German Renaissance style, introduced for the first time in this Colony'. The upper storey with its 'quaint dormer windows, pediments, Mansard roof, and capola [cupola]' and tower were removed in later years and its 'red pointed brickwork and artificial stone facings' have long since been plastered over.

The Cape Argus

The original construction was to a plan by the Dutch architect, Anthony De Witt, who came to South Africa in 1879. William Black, an Australian architect, undertook extensions in about 1900. The prominent verandah that is shown in early drawings on both the Long and Castle Street façades was supported originally on cast-iron columns. During a rebuild, possibly in the 1920s, the verandah was re-erected on four sets of concrete pillars on Long Street only. The projecting concrete balconettes and window hoods on the upper floors also probably date from this time.

Although situated in the same block as the YMCA, the hotel was largely ignored by YM residents in the 1950s, as most of us could just about afford our board-and-lodging at the YM, let alone 'eat out'. In later years, however, when I worked in Bree Street, lunching on the hotel's enclosed terrace became extremely popular with Capetonians during weekdays and it was necessary to arrive early to ensure a lunchtime view of the passing traffic below in Long Street. Recently upgraded, the hotel ranks as one of the city's top hotels and continues its proud tradition of providing fine accommodation and cuisine for locals and tourists.

Above:
No. 38, in 1895
Opposite:
No. 38, today

Desmond Martin

No. 40 Long Street
SA Slave Church (Museum) or SA Sendinggestig
(South African Missionary Society)

The Sendinggestig is the oldest indigenous mission in South Africa having been established in 1799. The church was built between 1802 and 1804 by 'the master mason, Johan Godfried Mocke and the master carpenter, Joseph van Schalkoven. The façade was designed by FW de Wet' (D Picton-Seymour, *Historical Buildings in South Africa*, Struikhof, 1989). It was the first church to be built in the form of a basilica with a curved apsidal end. In addition to the divine services for its members, the church provided religious and literacy instruction for slaves and non-Christians at the Cape.

During my days at the YMCA I recall that the church was well attended but apparently in the 1960s, as the congregation began to be re-settled on the Cape Flats, the building became dilapidated. In 1971 it was sold and in danger of being demolished. In 1977 the Sendinggestig was proclaimed a national monument and, financed by the Cape Provincial authorities and under the direction of architect Dirk Visser, it was fully restored. It is now the South African Slave Church Museum and a 'must see' in Long Street. The interior is beautifully furnished with carved oak pews, decorated pipe organ and a fine Neo-classical pulpit with two staircases. On display in the museum is an old photograph that shows Long Street buildings, Nos. 40, 42 and 44 as they were in 1884.

Take time, too, to appreciate the magnificent exterior that features four tall Corinthian pilasters, a broad dentilled cornice and a concave-shaped Cape gable with a circular ventilator and four urns on the skyline. To the left of the church is an old warehouse, once part of the church property and now Gordon's Hardware (No. 42). The warehouse that incorporated the church caretaker's dwelling was given a pediment some time after 1884.

Opposite: *No. 40*

No. 44/48 Long Street *(see also illustration on page 8)*

Old YMCA (currently Cofida Caffe)

Originally the YMCA building comprised three storeys. It was built in 1883 to a design by Charles Freeman, the architect of a number of Cape Town's important buildings including the Metropolitan Methodist Church on Greenmarket Square. In 1900 a fourth storey was added and a stairway and substantial extensions built on the Hout Street side where the foundation stone can still be seen at the side entrance. It reads: *'Young Men's Christian Association. Founded in Cape Town 24th August 1865. Building erected 1883 and extended 1900. This stone was laid by His Excellency the Governor, Sir Alfred Milner GCMG KCB on 4th October 1900. 1 Peter 2.6.'* The biblical reference quoted reads: *'See, I lay a stone in Zion, a chosen and precious cornerstone, and the one who trusts in him will never be put to shame.'(NIV)*

As shown in my watercolour opposite, a double-storey verandah still dominates the façade on Long Street. A steep staircase leads immediately up from the entrance of polished granite to the first floor landing where double doors open into the Oak Hall (adjoining the YMCA in Hout Street as shown in the watercolour on page 8) that became the Space Theatre in the late 1970s. The entire front of the building is covered in a rich mix of windows in groups of twos and threes, elaborate plasterwork and applied decoration. Notice the broad ledge between the third and fourth floors that was the main cornice at parapet level prior to the extensions of 1900.

My anecdotes in the foreword, 'I lived in Long Street', describe life at the YMCA in the 1950s. The YM continued to provide accommodation for young men during the 1960s but very early in the 1970s the YM moved to smaller premises in Queen Victoria Street. With the coming in the late 1970s of new tenants, the Space Theatre (that had begun in 1972 in Upper Long Street), the building entered a new phase of 'service'. The YMCA had been dedicated in 1885 and again in 1900 to help young white men 'find their way' in the city. About 80 years later young black men were able to use the stage in the Oak Hall to act out pleas for a democratic South Africa that became a reality in 1994. For these reasons alone the old YMCA deserves the City's special protection.

To the left of the YMCA in my watercolour is a seven-storey concrete framed building (No. 50) that has some intricate plaster drapery decorations in the spaces between the windows on the sixth storey. It is a pity that being so high above the street, few people can appreciate this fine Art Deco work from the 1930s.

Opposite:
No. 44/48

Desmond Martin

Desmond Martin

No. 51 Long Street

Standard House (currently Castle Street Backpackers)

Despite this building being more in Castle Street than in Long Street, it also shows a charming face on the latter façade where the parapet features the date, 'AD 1902'. The original structure, however, was possibly built as early as the eighteenth century. With the unprecedented increase in tourism in Cape Town in recent decades I am glad to see that backpackers are currently bringing new life to some buildings in Long Street such as Standard House. Washing draped over the railings and drying in the sun is not an unwelcome sight!

The ground floor shopfronts may have changed since 1902 but the intriguing intersecting plasterwork on the upper floors on both façades is original and deserves more than a passing glance. Other aspects to note are the large-pane sash windows, the ornamental keystones above the first floor windows and the window surrounds (pilasters).

Each upper window on the Castle Street side is surmounted alternately by an inverted 'V' and a semi-circle while the upper windows overlooking Long Street are grouped in their own design under the date. The concrete and steel joist verandah, standing on three columns on Long Street and cantilevered over Castle Street, is neatly finished with a cast-iron railing. The plaster ornamentations, currently painted white, stand out well against the warm apricot colour of the walls.

To the right of Standard House in my illustration is No. 53 Long Street, formerly Western Province House. Originally this was a plain Victorian three-storey building dating from the 1850s. It has been altered several times but most of the cast-iron verandah survives. The recent use of the orange and white colour scheme allows this building to blend in with others of similar vintage in the street.

Opposite: *No. 51, corner of Castle and Long Streets (the narrow, front façade faces onto Long Street)*

Desmond Martin

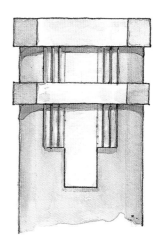

No. 55 Long Street
D. M. Murray & Co (Pty) Ltd

This late 1930s three-storey building, still with its original name across the upper façade, exhibits a number of Art Deco features. These include the moulded plastered concrete verandah with its two concave corners, the four recessed arched bays that enclose the windows and the row of squares running across the top of the building. The projecting lift tower on the left is subtly stepped at the top thus softening the impact of the tower on the bulk of the building currently painted in pale peppermint green with white trim. Spot the subtle Art Deco designs at the top of the two verandah pillars.

The ground floor was used for years by Crawford's Carpet and Linoleum Company. I recall that in the 1950s a long wooden counter ran the full length of the shop to facilitate displaying carpets to customers. As a YMCA resident I had no reason to visit Crawford's but I always enjoyed the pleasant smell of new carpets that wafted into Long Street.

Depicted on the right in the illustration is Caldis House, formerly Benson House, No. 57A Long Street. There is archival evidence that the original structure was a fine three-storey Victorian building that was subsequently given a fourth floor (Rennie survey). Notice the 'backward stepping parapet' at the top of the building and the curved heads of the first and second floor windows. My watercolour on page 39 gives another view of Caldis House, to the left of No. 59.

Above:
Detail of Art Deco verandah pillar
Opposite: *No. 55, centre building in the illustration*

No. 59 Long Street *(cnr of Hout Street)*

Langham House (formerly the Langham Hotel)

Though the 'Langham' is no longer a hotel, the building still has the air of the quiet boarding house where the more elderly, moneyed folk used to end their days in comfort. At least this is the opinion I held of its residents as I stood on the YMCA verandah across the street in 1954/55 and caught glimpses of the Langham's patrons.

The hotel was built in the early 1940s as the lift is dated 1941. The Langham's most attractive feature is its two-storey verandah that stands on small brick (faggot) piers with sandstone bases above the pavement (sidewalk). In its earlier days it was enclosed and a pleasant spot to dine when the winter sun was low in the sky. The walls are of red facebrick up to first floor level, then plastered for two storeys with bands of brick on the top floor. In contrast with the flat roofs and windows of the buildings around it, the sloping red tile roofs and timber shutters of the Langham add to its mellow suburban character.

Read for yourself the bronze plaque in the small entrance on the left in Long Street. It states that the original erf was granted in 1698 by Governor Simon van der Stel. A private dwelling was on the site for decades and at some stage it was converted into a hotel. Then in 1890 Ohlssons Cape Breweries bought the hotel and rebuilt it in 1928 (the ground floor plus three floors above it). Three years later the top floor was added. The hotel stopped trading as a hotel in 1959, four years after I left the YMCA so I am glad I remember it in its heyday. Thereafter the well-known music shop, Hans Kramer, operated from what was originally the first floor dining room.

Langham House became very neglected in the 1980s but was restored to its original splendour by the current owners, the Van Nieuwenhuisens, between 1993 and 1995. The original teak staircase, windows, brass fittings and lift have all been retained. Do yourself a favour and enjoy the taste and aroma of the Langham House coffee bar on the ground floor and while you are there let your gaze drift across Long Street to my old home on the opposite side, the YMCA.

The view of the Langham in my watercolour is unique in that I was able to take the photograph in June 2005, soon after the original Carnarvon House on the corner of Hout Street had been demolished to make way for a new development. Within months, as the successor began to rise up, this once-in-a-lifetime view was obliterated. To the left of the hotel is Caldis House, described on page 37.

Opposite: *No. 59*

Desmond Martin

No. 68 Long Street

Shap's Cameraland (formerly Shap's Central Pharmacy)

It is only when one draws or paints a Victorian building such as this corner beauty, that you begin to appreciate just how much ornamentation can be incorporated on a building's elevation. Take time to view the wavy parapet with its nine small gablets, the lavish decoration of each window framed between fluted surrounds. Notice too the balconettes with their cast-iron railings that are supported on decorated concrete brackets. These link the top floor windows with those on the first floor; the latter carry an intricate design within a plaster arch above the window.

The building's splayed corner was given extra attention by the architect William Black in 1900 when extensive alterations were made and the corner turret added. Plaster quoins on the upper floors flank the single window on the first floor and the unusual projecting plaster design on the second floor. The corner treatment terminates in an attractive octagonal turret with a slate pinnacle and flagpole. Note how the shafts of the supporting columns are interrupted by square blocks, a device repeated in the window surrounds.

In its earlier days the building had a short verandah on Long Street that was accessed through the two first floor doors to the right of the corner. Despite the loss of the verandah and the extensive alterations to the ground floor, the building is a delightful example of its time. The photographic business operating on the premises was founded by Gerald Shap in 1958 and has maintained this property in good condition ever since. Inside the photo shop is a restored imported pine staircase that is worth a look.

In the foyer of the adjoining building in my watercolour (No. 66, Park-On-Long) is a display of old photographs and a history of Long Street prepared by the Archaeology Department of the University of Cape Town. A section of early local 'blue stone' walling from the eighteenth century and an early brick wall and beam are also on display. Sealed but visible in the floor of the foyer is a time capsule that is scheduled to be opened on 1 January 2100!

Opposite: *No. 68*

Desmond Martin

Desmond Martin

No. 72/74 Long Street *(cnr of Shortmarket Street)*

Winchester House (Tribal Trends, formerly the Swiss Tea Room)

How often I walked past the old Swiss Tea Room on the corner of this building during my days at the YM, longing to indulge myself with creamy Swiss confectionery and some continental coffee. But my student's purse was too small and my fear of being 'short' at month-end, too great. So I never enjoyed what the tearoom could offer and today it is no more.

Winchester House, designed by John Lyon in 1903, is an impressive Edwardian four-storey corner building with an attic and an octagonal corner turret. Rising behind and almost level with the turret is its steeply pitched roof of Welsh slate. Since the 1950s the ground floor has been changed a few times though recent slim cast-iron columns still support the handsomely railed first floor verandah. In 1990, as I mentioned earlier when I wrote about the conservation of Long Street, the building was at the centre of controversy as a result of the total gutting of the inside floors. I recall how the façade was soundly secured by scaffolding while the core of the building was being removed and the rubble carted away. Despite the loss of all that was architecturally valuable on the inside, Winchester House still appears on the outside as it was when it was built. The original timber shopfront on the corner is well preserved.

The building has a diversity of decorative plasterwork: its three floors of windows and doors are delineated by ornamented plaster surrounds; above the cornice, six gabled dormer windows lend a Dutch touch to the structure while an intricate floral design is emblazoned on the third floor chamfer panel. Unlike other corner buildings, Winchester House has matching façades on both street fronts, a symmetry that I think imparts an air of dignity to the overall design.

The building, depicted in my watercolour in a cheerful colour scheme of cream and sea green, was subsequently redecorated in a sombre battleship grey.

Opposite:
No. 72/74

Desmond Martin

No. 76/80 Long Street
The Pan African Market (formerly the YWCA)

The old YWCA, as related in my preamble, was well known to the young men from the YM. Blinded by the close proximity of young ladies at the YW Sunday tea parties, I did not at the time appreciate the architectural beauties around me. The entrance lobby, for example, apart from its teak doors, is decorated with shiny Victorian tiles in panels of rusty brown and aquamarine blue. These may be seen as you make your way to the African market on the first floor.

The building is an exceptionally fine example of the work of the architect John Parker of the firm Parker and Forsyth. It comprises four storeys: a ground floor with a heavy cast-iron, double-level verandah accessible from the first and second floors, and a third floor, all under a steeply pitched tiled roof. In the 1950s the second floor railing incorporated the full title, YOUNG WOMEN'S CHRISTIAN ASSOCIATION in cast-iron letters. The two gable ends of the building terminate in chimney stacks, each with three pots, building features that are fairly rare in the city.

The architect has utilized a wide range of ornamental devices to decorate the façade. Notice on the third floor the fine plaster pulvinated (convex) frieze supported on modillions and below it, a cornice with an egg-and-dart pattern. Four banded pilasters and two slim columns divide the face of the building into five panels (bays). The columns in the centre stand on twisted 'barley-sugar' columns that flank the commemorative panel, the focal point of the building. This reads: '*In memory of Minnie & Maria Bam, Founded 1886, rebuilt 1903.*' The teenage Bam sisters died of enteric fever in 1886, soon after arriving in Germany after sailing from Cape Town. Their father, Johannes Andries Bam, donated his Long Street house in their memory to establish a YWCA in the city. Bam's original house was demolished and the present building erected on the site. An archival photograph of the building with three storeys and different cast-iron work and detailing is further evidence that the top floor was added later, together with all the other modifications (Rennie survey).

The humble two-storey building on the left in my watercolour, No. 84, FORK, though 'modernized' through the years is suspected to contain old building fabric. Old teak shopfittings are still visible on the ground floor.

Opposite:
No. 76/80

Desmond Martin

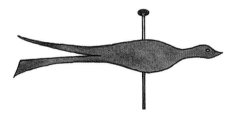

No. 89 Long Street *(cnr of Shortmarket)*

The Purple Turtle (formerly the Green Hansom, the Imperial Hotel)

Designed in 1901 by the architects Parker and Forsyth, this charming corner hotel has been a landmark in Long Street for over a century. The completion date, '1902', can be seen on the centre shield just below the second storey window on the far right of the building. Below it is a rampant lion, symbol of the Ohlsson's Cape Brewery that linked a number of Cape Town's hotels at the time.

The hotel has changed its name and livery at least twice since the 1950s. In the 1970s it became the Green Hansom Restaurant and was painted a dark green with its fine plaster ornamentation picked out in white. Round about the late 1980s the old hotel stunned Capetonians when it became the Purple Turtle with an equally provocative colour scheme to match. Currently one of the city's 'drinking holes', I doubt whether patrons have the time to appreciate the building's unusual architectural features. These include balconettes (small concrete balconies) and pilasters on the third floor façade, the double oval ground floor corner windows set into the sandstone walling and the octagonal four-storey tower with its shingled domed roof. The weathervane in the shape of a goose in flight is still there. Notice too the Art Nouveau ironwork of the balconies and the four-sided finial on the roof of the tower.

The tall building in my watercolour looming up to the left and behind the Purple Turtle should not be missed if you have the time to make a short detour down Shortmarket Street to Greenmarket Square. Avoid all the tempting bargains of the open market fronting the building and stand well back in the centre of the square. Look up at the impressive bulk of the symmetrical building in front of you and you will be looking at the old Shell House that was modelled on Shell Mex House on the Thames Embankment, London. The South African version was designed in the 1920s by the architect WH Grant. The building was erected in two stages, in 1929 and in 1941. You can return to Long Street by walking up Longmarket Street to the left of 'Shell House'.

Above: *Detail of weathervane*

Opposite: *No. 89*

No. 90 Long Street

Unity House (Mali South Trading, Long Street Books)

This three-storey Edwardian corner building, dating from about 1900, has matching façades on both Long and Longmarket Streets except for the gable on the Long Street face (on the left). The focal point is undoubtedly the entire four-storey corner of the building that reminds me of a minaret on a mosque. The 'Indian' character in the treatment of the turret's roof was commented on in the 1977 survey. Its curved, bulbous dome is echoed in the curves of the oriel window above the splayed corner entrance. The Eastern feel continues on the upper floor with its profusion of plasterwork that includes, on both street fronts, three large-paned sash windows flanked with columns and set under a heavy dentilled projecting eaves.

Although the ground floor façade has been altered during the years, the Cape granite of the supporting piers can still be seen. At the time of doing my watercolour all the plasterwork was painted white against a cheerful background of yellow ochre, a colour scheme that effectively shows off the elaborate treatment of the walls.

On the opposite corner (just showing on the right) is No. 86/88 Long Street, now Skinz Leatherware. This three-storey building dates from about 1935 and exhibits some typical Art Deco characteristics. These include the three bays above Long Street that are separated by plain pilasters, the unadorned parapet and the criss-cross motif used both on the windows and the wrought-iron railing on the canopy above the ground floor.

Opposite: No. 90 with Longmarket Street on the right

Desmond Martin

Desmond Martin

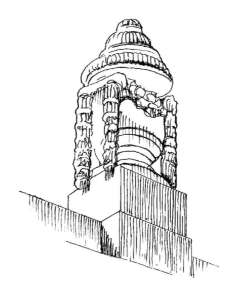

No. 100 Long Street

First National Bank (formerly Barclays National Bank)

Classical Greek columns have always suggested to me that a building has a formal function such as a law court or a city hall. This bank building with its symmetrical façade and Corinthian columns exudes the same air of authority. Since my YMCA days when no YM resident darkened the door of a bank, banks have become much more friendly. Maybe the warm orange colour now used for the walls, for decades painted a pristine white, is an attempt by the bankers to temper the stern exterior of the building.

Designed by architect Gordon Leith in about 1935, the building includes classical and Italianate elements such as the two tall columns and the half-round windows with prominent keystones and voussoirs on the Long Street front (on the right in my illustration). The Church Street façade (on the left) boasts four columns with the bank windows set back. Notice the enormous Cape granite stones used for the base and the balustrade, and ornamental urns above the cornice. Balcony railings and gates are of wrought iron and windows are of teak.

Above:
Ornamental
Classical urn
Opposite: *No. 100*

Desmond Martin

No. 107/111 Long Street

Portobello Café (and an antique shop)

The following two buildings in my watercolour, Nos. 107 and 113, complement each other in a number of ways: they have very similar dentilled cornices, each surmounted by a parapet with a dominant centrepiece. I like to think that when the architect added the top storey to No. 113 (Windsor House – on the right) in 1922, he took into consideration the features of no. 107 that had been remodelled some 20 or more years earlier.

The original No. 107 two-storey building was probably completed in the 1860s, though, when first surveyed by Rennie, some eighteenth century windows were found at the back on the upper floor. It is thought that the elaborate cornice with the central open pediment (painted in white), the additional panelled parapet (painted in green) and yet another pediment above it were added in the 1890s. Note the large cast-iron verandah columns supporting the balcony with a delicate leaf design in the iron railing. Inside the shop on the left there are large cast-iron supporting columns that feature ancient Egyptian designs on their capitals and bases.

No. 113/115 Long Street (cnr of Church Street)

Windsor House (Aspen Florists, Sterling Antiques, Mesopotamia Restaurant)

The date '1922' on the rectangular pediment of Windsor House indicates that the third floor was added on to the two-storey building that is visible in an old panorama photo taken in c.1859. Notice that, being a 1920s rebuild, the parapet and balcony wall are decorated with rectangular panels of the period. The concrete verandah with its four sets of twin concrete columns is more distinctly 1920/1930.

The verandah is currently partially covered by the orange canvas awning of the first floor restaurant. The corner of the building on the right has a 45° chamfer as it turns into Church Street where there is an entrance to the upstairs restaurant. Unlike many other shopfronts in Long Street that have been 'modernized', the slender teak frames of the original shopfronts can still be admired.

Opposite:
Nos. 107/111
and 113/115
(on the right)

Desmond Martin

No. 108 Long Street *(and 41 Church Street)*

Scott House (Mister Music, Tribe Café, formerly the old Johannesburg Hotel)

Currently sporting a scarlet and white colour scheme, this three-storey building was probably built in the 1880s. In my YMCA days of 1955 I vaguely recall it having a single coach lamp that burnt dimly above the narrow central entrance on Long Street. I believe it functioned then as the old Johannesburg Hotel, one of the many Lion Hotels of the era.

At the time of the Rennie survey of 1977, the hotel had already closed and the building's ground floor had been 'modernized' with plate glass windows, though the upper two floors remained undisturbed, retaining their large-pane sash windows. The Victorian plastered architraves, small concrete balcony above the entrance and wrought-iron railings are also the original fabric and, significantly, the heraldic rampant lion in its ornamented frame still has pride of place on the Long Street façade. As late as 2005 the doorway was bricked-up. With the coming of the coffee shop on the corner in 2006, the doorway was re-opened thus restoring the emphasis on the centrepoint of the symmetrical façade.

To the left of the hotel is No. 110, currently Space Station Clothing. Although there was a three-storey building on this site c.1900, the present four-storey building of painted facebrick probably dates from the 1930s, as evidenced by a number of Art Deco features.

Above: *Decorative pediment above centre window*
Opposite: *No. 108*

Desmond Martin

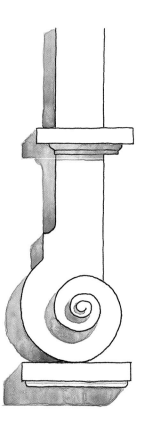

Above: *Two-metre tall volute on second floor*
Left: *No. 112*

No. 112 Long Street

Twinell Building (formerly the Central News Agency store)

This tall warehouse was designed by John Parker (1866–1921) in about 1920, the date noted on the building's lift by Rennie during his inspection in 1977. The warehouse comprises a ground floor and six upper floors, as well as an attic set in the gable.

Note how the architect framed the four middle floors between two prominent extended pilasters that terminate in two giant volutes. Notice too how the long keystones of the three semi-circular arches link the lower floor to the upper floors. Smaller volutes, circles and rusticated plaster decorate the top floor and attic reminiscent of old Dutch townhouses of Amsterdam. An early photograph shows that a smaller gable (now removed) surmounted the uppermost cornice (refer line sketch). The structure's red facebrick walls, currently painted in a dark purple/blue with the decorative plasterwork in white, makes a bold statement on Long Street.

Above: *Attic showing the smaller gable before removal*

No. 117 Long Street *(Church Street on the left)*

Imagenius (formerly Peter Visser Antiques, EK Green & Co Bottle Store)

Described nearly 30 years ago by Rennie as a 'late Victorian showpiece', this is surely the quaintest corner building in the whole of Long Street. A life-size statue of a young lady is given centre stage in the oriel window above the corner and has been gazing wistfully onto the open-air antiques market for decades. The two steep gables, one above Church and the other above Long Street, are identical and are roofed with slate. The first floor walls are extensively decorated with twin pilasters, window hoods and trims and an ornate cornice. Fruit and foliage devices can be seen on the capitals of the pilasters and in the plasterwork below the windows.

When the building was the Peter Visser shop, it was painted dark red and white; the current bottle green and white, however, is no less attractive. An intriguing feature is the seven wrought-iron strainer bars from which is hung the corrugated-iron canopy shading the pavement. Teak doors and old shop fittings are still to be seen on the ground floor while inside the shop are a cast-iron spiral staircase and embossed ceilings. It was thought that the architect was probably Anthony De Witt, as he designed many of EK Green's buildings in Cape Town but the original 1899 plans reveal that the architect was RM Robertson who also designed EK Green's large warehouse in Somerset Road, Green Point.

No. 119/121 Long Street *(on the right in the illustration)*

Fotokino Photoshop

This building, designed in 1899 by the architect William Black, is a matched pair of Victorian shops. Each shop has a pedimented dormer window in the steep, tiled roof and an elaborate balustraded parapet above a single, centre, sash window. Dating from about 1859, this building was subsequently developed into its paired form when the dormer windows were also added.

A corrugated-iron canopy standing on six slender, decorated, cast-iron columns shades the pavement and windows from the warm afternoon sun. The decorative ironwork at the top of the columns is particularly fine. Unfortunately the mass of the adjoining high-rise office block (No. 127) tends to overshadow this little building so that it can easily be overlooked.

Opposite:
Nos. 117
and 119/121
(on the right)

Desmond Martin

No. 127/137 Long Street *(cnr of No. 38 Wale Street)*
Wale Street Chambers (formerly African Homes Trust)

An impressive bas-relief elephant head in pink granite looks down from this 11-storey concrete-framed office block onto Wale Street just around the corner from Long Street. The work is by the well-known Cape Town sculptor, Ivan Mitford Barberton. Wale Street Chambers was completed in the late 1950s for the African Homes Trust for which an elephant head was the corporate symbol. Coincidentally, Long Street was apparently known in its earliest days as 'Elephant Street'.

Although the building did not exist when I was at the YMCA in 1954/55, I can clearly recall the impressive deep excavation on the site. I would walk past this gaping hole on Long Street every Sunday morning on the way to the old Cape Town (Wale Street) Baptist Church (No. 36 Wale Street) where a number of the YM lads, including my brother and I, worshipped regularly. In the absence of a corner building, *the sidewall* of the church faced Long Street. Considering too that the old church played a significant spiritual role during my year in Long Street, I have given it 'honorary Long Street status'.

Its history is also fascinating, as two renowned Cape Town personalities, Thomas Bowler (artist) and Charles Freeman (architect), were associated with the building.

My watercolour of the church is based on a *Cape Times* photograph from February 1965. It shows the African Homes Trust with the elephant head on the left and, on the right, the modified School of Art building that the Baptists purchased from Mr A Madirose in February 1880. Charles Freeman was appointed by the church leaders as the architect to add a hall at the rear of the premises and to modify the existing school to function as a church. Freeman retained the Italianate style of the frontage of the building and it served the Cape Town

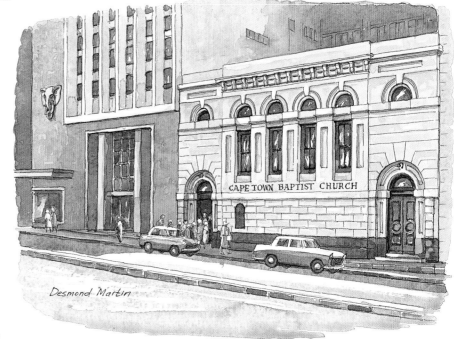

Desmond Martin

Desmond Martin

Left: *Bas-relief elephant on No. 127*
Opposite: *The old Wale Street Baptist Church, 1965*

Baptists from March 1882 until 1965 when the congregation moved to their present premises in Orange Street. The old church was demolished soon afterwards and a four-storey building was erected c.1970 for IBM and subsequently used by the Owen Wiggins Trust. When Rennie surveyed the building in 1977 he noted that small plaques at the entrance carried the following inscription: 'Thomas William Bowler (1812-1869), Best known Cape Artist of the Nineteenth Century lived from 31st January 1861 until his death in 1869 in a house that stood on this site.'

The Owen Wiggins building was later superseded by the Long Street Arcade but the plaques referring to Bowler have, unhappily, disappeared. I find that the present arcade, crammed with antiques, bric-a-brac and books is a fascinating but restful place to have coffee – on the very site where I attended church in 1954/55.

THE AFRICAN MUSIC STORE

134

Desmond Martin

The buildings of
Upper Long Street

No. 134/136 Long Street
The African Music Store, Daddy Longlegs Hotel

The centre building in my illustration was formerly the home of Arthur Elliot. A brass plaque, long since disappeared, carried the following inscription: '*On this site lived Arthur Elliot, an American Gentleman who made the Cape his home and The Record of Her History in photographs his life work. 1870 – 1936.*' The South African architect Johann E Seeliger is also known to have had rooms in the building in the early 1900s.

It is easy to see why Arthur Elliot selected this compact building for his residence and photographic studio. The concrete verandah, supported by three cast-iron columns, provides shade on the ground floor business area and provided a comfortable area for relaxing after hours. (It is currently used by the hotel as an extension of the first floor cocktail lounge.) Two banded pilasters framing the symmetrical façade of the two upper floors become the side gable ends of the high-pitched tiled roof with two dormer windows. Other doors and windows are framed in broad plaster surrounds.

Centre of interest is the elegant second floor balcony, which is surmounted by a plaster shield (escutcheon), a semi-circular hood mould and, above these, the plaster panel with the date '1903'. The steep gable lends a touch of the Cape Dutch style to the building, declared a national monument by the NMC in 1985.

The buildings on either side of No. 134 cannot be overlooked. No. 138 (Rcaffé) to the left, built probably in the 1930s and now painted in a canary yellow, has four polished black granite columns supporting a substantial concrete verandah. The upper floor has three teak windows and doors, each set within stylized plaster surrounds and a prominent plaster cornice and pediment that run the length of the building. Not shown in my watercolour is the centre portion of the parapet with its pair of finely moulded anthemion motifs and a flagstaff.

The cheerful peach-coloured building on the right, No. 128/130 (Tommy's Booksellers and Alternative Design), is a good example of the Art Deco style that is characterized by unadorned flat surfaces and clean, straight lines. Probably built about 1940, the symmetrical façade comprises two outer panels (bays) that rise to a stepped parapet while two middle panels are recessed in three stages on either side of a central flat pilaster. Dark timber windows contrast strongly against the peach colour of the façade with selected panels highlighted in white.

No. 138 Long Street *(cnr of Long and Dorp Streets)*
Noor El Hamedia Mosque (known as the Dorp Street Mosque)

Dating from 1884, the Dorp Street Mosque shows both Victorian and Eastern architectural influences in the horseshoe-shaped doors and windows. The horseshoe arch is a typical feature in Islamic architecture, as is the minaret, built in this instance in an octagonal shape with an onion-shaped roof.

Delicate plaster shafts flank all the windows as well as the main entrance and the door to the small minaret. Note the Arabic-engraved marble plaques fixed above the doors on both the Long and Dorp Street façades. The latter plaque carries the full name of the building in Arabic as well as the date, 'Est. 1884'. Walls are plastered and painted in yellow ochre with the decorative features highlighted in white.

I was amazed to discover that the mosque and its neighbour on the right, Rcaffé, both display the street number (No. 138), an anomaly that appears not to interfere with the two buildings' distinct functions.

Above: *Applied plaster decoration above door and front windows*
Opposite: *No. 138*

Desmond Martin

Desmond Martin

No. 140 Long Street

Tyne Buildings

This is the first of a trio of late nineteenth century buildings that were proclaimed national monuments by the old NMC in May 1991. Occupying the righthand side of Long Street between Dorp and Leeuwen Streets, their restoration was termed 'a breakthrough for conservation in the city' (D Picton-Seymour, *Historical Buildings in South Africa*, Struikhof, 1989). Tyne Buildings as it now appears was completed in about 1900, though the site had already been developed in the 1860s. Yellowwood and stinkwood floorboards and ceiling beams discovered during restoration indicate even earlier beginnings.

The building's name is inscribed in plaster letters on the partially balustraded parapet but apart from the two small festoons below the moulded cornice, decoration of the façade is restrained. The first floor is neatly edged with plaster quoins. A feature of the building is the balustraded open verandah (added later in about 1925) that curves gracefully around the splayed corner. Verandah doors and windows, and ground floor shop fronts are of teak.

No. 142 Long Street

Cape Gateway (formerly Dorfman & Katz Furnishers)

Despite the 'ESTB. 1898' inscribed on its high parapet, this building originally comprised two smaller buildings, one with three windows (on the right) and the other with two. These nineteenth century buildings were amalgamated as one in about 1920 during which process the façade was remodelled and a verandah added to the first floor. Notice that the verandah door, the second from the right, is set in a slightly projecting panel. A dentilled cornice runs between the windows of the first and second floors. There are some expensive touches in the ground floor materials: the polished granite bases of the six verandah columns, the marble and teak in the shop fronts and the Art Deco 'radiating sun' design in blue and white glass of the upper shopfront windows.

Above: *Detail of Art Deco window on No. 142*
Opposite:
Nos. 140 and 142 (on the left)

Desmond Martin

No. 148 Long Street

Wiener Building (Delizio Deli and Public Works information office)

One of the finest late Victorian buildings in Cape Town, the Wiener Bakery as it was known, was completed in 1902 as confirmed by the date on the pediment of the middle gable. The bakery was established three years later. There are indications that the building originally had a two-storey verandah. This was removed and replaced by the present concrete verandah, probably in the 1930s. The elaborate plasterwork, decorated cornice, fluted pilasters and plaster window surrounds, corner turret and attic windows are all typical of the period.

Although the Wiener Bakery was situated five city blocks away from the YMCA at 44 Long Street, it was recognized by the forever hungry YM residents in the 1950s as their 'back-up' source of food. I recall a few occasions in 1954 and 1955 when a birthday was celebrated that doughnuts, sticky buns and cream cakes were purchased at Wieners and carried back to the 'Y' for the feast.

The building was completely restored by the Cape Provincial Administration in 1982, giving the lead to other bodies for conservation of similar historic buildings in the street. Particularly noteworthy is the judicious use of lemon, lilac and white as a colour scheme that emphasizes the various architectural features of the façades.

Above: *Decorated window pediment*
Opposite: *No. 148*

No. 175/177 Long Street *(Leeuwen Street on the right in illustration)*

Arcmen House (Red Moon Coffee Shop and Bristol Antiques)

Designed by the Australian architect William Black in 1898, this beautiful Victorian corner office was in grave danger of collapse in the 1980s. Encouraged by the Institute of Architects at the time to promote architecture as a whole, a firm of local architects, Meiring and Naudé, purchased the building in 1985 and decided to restore the building to its early glory. The project, headed by architect Thomas Geh, was completed nine months later in 1986.

Among the many repairs undertaken at the time, the dilapidated two-storey balcony of cast iron was replaced with an aluminium railing identical to the original design. The seven attic windows, heavily encrusted with plaster pediments, cornices and flanking volutes, are still the crowning glory of the building. Note the date, 1898, on the windowsill of the corner attic window.

To the left of Arcmen House is '169-on-long', a seven-bay Victorian building that also boasts a double-storey cast-iron covered verandah. The design of the ornamental railings, probably not the original fabric, are every bit as authentic as the Victorian designs further up the street. Notice the three subtle steps on either side of the centre panel of the long parapet that break the monotony of an otherwise plain parapet across the top of the building.

Above: *'Broekie lace' on cast-iron column* Opposite: *No. 175/177*

Martin

1898

No. 178/182 Long Street (cnr of Pepper Street)

Mama Africa

When the architect A Benning altered the existing two-storey building in 1899 for the owner, Mr G van Heerde, he added a two-storey cast-iron and timber verandah supported on cast-iron columns on both street fronts. Delicately patterned cast-iron railings similar to those on No. 186/196 completed the picture. During the early 1900s Van Heerde ran the Star Grocery store on the corner. A taxi crashed into the supports in 1981 and much of the verandah collapsed. Tragically the structure and all its trimmings were removed immediately afterwards without considering temporary propping and repair.

The windows in the upper storey retain their original form; the three on the left have plaster surrounds and a prominent keystone while the trio on the right have curved heads. Paired consoles still support the original cornice.

Though the building looks nothing like it was when it was built (and as I vaguely remember it in the 1950s with its decorative railed verandah), it contributes an indigenous flavour to the trendy vibe of upper Long Street. Its Victorian parapet on the roofline and its walls are currently coloured in earthy, yellow ochre and tan complementing the black and tan of the ground floor and window surrounds and the three enormous African faces painted on the Pepper Street façade. The signage of the restaurant on the splayed corner completes the Afro-Victorian picture.

Opposite:
No. 178/182

Desmond Martin

Desmond Martin

No. 185 Long Street

The Palm Tree Mosque (Dadel-Boom Mosque)

The simple lines and unpretentious face of this building belies its fascinating and well-documented history. The house was built by Carel Lodewijk Schot between 1787 and 1790, probably as a single-storey dwelling. In 1807 it was bought by two Cape Muslims, Jan van Bougies (Boekies) and Frans van Bengalen. Four years later, Van Bougies became sole owner and some time between 1811 and 1821 it is thought that the upper storey was added when the house became a place of worship for the Muslim community. (Refer to *The Old Buildings of the Cape*, p.52.) It is therefore one of the oldest mosques in Cape Town.

Notice that the windowsills of the ground floor are just 30 centimetres above the pavement. The door and fanlight are also unusually low. These phenomena are attributed to the gradual rise in the level of Long Street over nearly two hundred years. The sash windows are typical eighteenth century Cape windows with small panes. From as early as 1884 photographs show a palm tree or two growing in front of the house though the tree presently gracing the frontage dates from the 1960s. A section of the palm tree removed in 1991 has been preserved.

The mosque is sandwiched between two twentieth century buildings, Palm House ('Studios on Long') on the right, an unattractive four-storey concrete frame building, and on the left, the old Drommedaris Hotel ('No. 5 Leeuwen Street'), built in the 1950s in a dark, rustic facebrick. Though a relative newcomer to Long Street, this former hotel is not out of scale with the older buildings around it. Its asymmetrical façade with the set-back section above the five-arched arcade on Leeuwen Street makes a brave attempt to add to the appeal of the intersection.

Opposite: *No. 185*

Desmond Martin

No. 186/196 Long Street

Zula Sound Bar *et al*

This double-storey Victorian building with its two-storey, cast-iron and timber verandah was saved from certain demolition in 1982 when it was provisionally declared a national monument by the NMC. If you stand too close admiring the cast-iron railings of the first floor you will certainly miss the building's crowning glory, a double-layered Victorian parapet above the corrugated roof of the verandah. Judging by the building to the left that has a similar design on its parapet, No. 186 probably also carried precast urns on the seven pedestals visible on the skyline. Rennie noted raised side parapets as well which suggest that the building had a flat roof when it was built in c.1859.

Public entrance to the upper floor and verandah of the Zula Sound Bar is via the left-hand door between the modern shop fronts on street level. If you climb the old timber stairs to visit the restaurant, note the encaustic tiled threshold at the entrance. Windows and doors on the balcony have prominent plaster surrounds and the walls are rusticated. The intricate patterned railings are typical of the period (see illustration on right) and can be inspected at close range on the balcony while you also enjoy the elevated views of Long Street.

To the left in my watercolour is another two-storey building, No. 198/202 Long Street, with a Victorian parapet, cornice and urns but with a concrete verandah in the style of the 1920s/1930s. Look out for the large, leaded fanlight above the doors on the ground floor. Raised side parapets again suggest that the original structure, built about 1859, had a flat roof.

Above: *Detail of patterned railing*
Opposite:
No. 186/196

No. 195/197 and No. 199/205 Long Street

(cnrs of Venken Lane)

Traffic Clothing and Price Taylor *et al*

These two Victorian double-storey buildings, as evidenced by the dates displayed on their raised centre parapets, were erected in 1895 and 1896 respectively. The building on the left no longer has the original five cast-iron posts on the ground floor; these were replaced by five concrete columns, probably in the 1930s. Though the upper iron posts remain, the balusters in the verandah rail were also removed and replaced with a wooden railing. The large pane sash windows on the first floor and the plaster quoins as well as other features are original. (This building was being restored when I photographed it in late 2006; certain features now lost will no doubt make their reappearance in due course.)

The building on the right has withstood the passing of time far better than its neighbour. It can still boast having what Rennie judged in 1978 was 'the most delicately ornate' double-storey, cast-iron verandah in Long Street. The intricate designs of the first floor railing are complemented by the equally fine floral design in the 'broekie lace' above the six cast-iron columns supporting the verandah. Stand well back and notice the heavy cornice above the corrugated-iron roof and the parapet with its handsome centrepiece that displays the '1896' date in raised plaster numerals. The configuration of the windows is also more innovative than its partner, No. 195. Two large-pane sash windows are set on either side of a centre bay that has double doors opening onto the verandah, all under a segmented arch. Plaster hood moulds can also be seen above all the windows. Truly a gem of its time and despite 'modern' mosaics on the ground floor walls and its current somewhat dilapidated condition, No. 201 continues to impress with its symmetrical design and old-fashioned detailing.

Above: Detail of 'broekie lace' on verandah of No. 199/205
Opposite: Nos. 195/197 and 199/205 (on the right)

Desmond Martin

No. 206/208 Long Street *(cnr of Bloem Street)*

The Blue Lodge (Computeria Internet Café and Blue Mountain Backpackers)

When Rennie surveyed this Victorian masterpiece in 1978, he described its magnificent two-storey verandah as 'part missing and much dilapidated'. A newspaper report of 1982 stated, 'the balconies in particular were structurally unsafe.' The timely rescue from decay and ultimate demolition of the Blue Lodge during the mid 1980s is attributed to the collective efforts of the former National Monuments Council, Cape Heritage Trust, the owner Hans Brust and the architect David van den Heever.

The Lodge was built in two stages. Designed as a boarding house by Max Rosenberg in 1900, it was extended and completed in 1904 by Austin Cooke. Comprising three storeys and an attic, it is richly decorated from top to toe. Apart from the prominent florid cast-iron railings (see illustration above) on both verandahs that wrap around the building, note the pinnacles on the top of the nine attic window gablets, the broad window surrounds and plaster banding on the walls and finally the weathervane on the corner turret. Supporting the verandah are highly ornamented cast-iron columns.

The ground floor was modernized as early as the 1970s. Inside the building however, many of the Victorian features remain, such as the timber staircase and matchboard ceilings. After restoration in the 1980s the walls were painted in bright blue and white. Though the subsequent introduction of yellow in the 1990s has overcomplicated the façade, the Lodge is a strong contender for being the most famous building in the street.

Above: *Unique florid design of verandah railing*
Opposite:
No. 206/208

Desmond Martin

210 LONG ST.
BAOBAB MALL

Desmond Martin

No. 210 Long Street *(on the right in my watercolour)*

Baobab Mall (formerly the Novel Flats 1933)

Presuming you have just been enchanted by the Blue Lodge's intricate fairytale architecture on the corner of Long and Bloem Street, you may be forgiven for being unmoved by the conservative lines of this building. Built in 1933 as the Novel Flats, it is typical of the Art Deco style of that era. A cantilevered concrete balcony with a wrought-iron railing spans the entrance to the ground floor mall that in its earlier days was a motor showroom. To the left of the balcony is the original entrance to the flats that also had another entrance on Bloem Street. Notice the date '1933' above the door and the three stepped, vertical panels on the face of the building that terminate in smaller panels highlighted in white.

No. 216 Long Street

Poza 24h Mediterranean Food

I knew this building in the 1950s as a single-storey café where hungry YMCA lads could buy a bun or a cooldrink long after every other shop in Long Street had closed for the night. The present ground floor shop was possibly a rebuild in about 1900 of an earlier building on the site. With its ornate Victorian parapet that includes an urn at each end and an open pediment in the centre, the little shop has remained a landmark on the street for about 90 years.

In recent years another three floors were added to the original shop but these have been sensibly set back a metre so that the attractive pediment could be retained as a free-standing decoration over the old shop. I also suspect that the additional three floors were deliberately left plain by the architect to prevent a clash of style with the Victorian ground floor. The upper façade's only architectural elements, the windows, are small pane sliding sashes that match the style of windows in the adjacent buildings.

Opposite:
Nos. 210 (on the right) and 216

Desmond Martin

No. 211/213/215 Long Street
Clarke's Bookshop and Atkinson's Antiques

Though this two-storey bookshop presents an uninspiring face to passers-by, the original fabric of the building dates from the 1850s. Modernized in the post-1940s, the building now has steel windows and a suspended canopy over the pavement. The eight steel straps supporting the canopy are the only intrusion on the otherwise featureless façade.

Clarke's Bookshop has operated from this site for over 50 years. With the shelves bursting with every conceivable book on southern Africa, its unpretentious interior deserves a visit. The painted timber (matchboard) ceilings are visible clues to the building's nineteenth century beginnings. The adjoining shop has a wide range of antiques for sale, all displayed under a beautifully restored suspended yellowwood ceiling.

Don't miss the large, red post box ('pillar box') positioned on the sidewalk outside Clarke's. This carries the crown and 'GR' monogram, a reminder of the reign of King George V (1910–1936).

No. 217 Long Street
Nando's

When Rennie surveyed this building in 1977 it was a plain four-storey concrete-framed structure (built possibly in the 1930s) with large steel windows, a concrete verandah and columns. He noted that though the lift was dated '1929', the presence of some matchboard ceilings indicated a building of much earlier age.

In the 1990s the ugly façade was given a facelift in the post-modern style. The utilitarian factory windows on the two uppermost floors were converted into five windows on each floor with proportions echoing those of the Victorian buildings on the street. The uninteresting 1930s flat parapet was given a cornice divided in the middle by a date panel and above this, a parapet with a segmented arch. Notice the central section that visually links the parapet and floors together. These 1992 modifications I believe successfully integrate the 'modernized' building with its older neighbours, which is why I decided to illustrate it. Extensive changes to the ground floor were made to accommodate the Nando's Restaurant that opened in late 2006.

Opposite:
*Nos. 211/213/215
and 217*

No. 219/221/223/225 Long Street
Beads Merchants

Viewing old buildings when canvas blinds on the verandahs have been drawn down can be frustrating, as the windows and doors cannot be seen. I decided to paint this building as I saw it basking in the Cape afternoon sun, as this is what many visitors are likely to catch sight of when walking Long Street.

Notwithstanding the impressive two-storey, cast-iron verandah with its corrugated-iron roof and Victorian cast-iron railings and columns, the upper wall and plastered parapet is disappointingly plain. Rennie noted in 1977 that a cornice had recently collapsed, a partial explanation for the barren upper wall. There is much to see, however, on the ground floor. The recessed glassed doorway into Beads Merchants (No. 223), for example, is framed in teak with some delicately turned woodwork that the average bead shopper is unlikely to notice.

A photographic panorama taken about 1884 and consulted by Rennie shows a small two-storey residence and a warehouse on the site, which explains why he found even much older fabric in the building during his survey of 1977. As there are also very similar buildings lower down the street with dates 1895 and 1896 on their parapets, it is probable that this building is, in fact, a late nineteenth century structure as well.

Above: Detail of
'broekie lace'
on columns
Opposite:
No. 219/221/223/225

Desmond Martin

Desmond Martin

No. 226/228 Long Street *(cnr of Buiten Street)*
Lola's Café and Fiction Bar

This building celebrates its position on Long and Buiten Streets with verandah walls that curve gracefully around the corner. Three storeys above the street, an elaborate, small, gabled tower on the roofline gives further emphasis to the corner. The date '1902' is etched into the faces of this feature, flanked on each side with a balustraded parapet. Tall cast-iron columns stand on either side of the corner entrance to the restaurant. Other features include the rusticated walls of the first floor (a mock-brick pattern scored into the plaster) and the plaster quoining on the vertical edge of the building.

Some architectural features of this building mirror those of the Overseas Visitors' Club (No. 230) on the opposite corner. Apart from their rounded corners and the use of balustrades, notice how the precast concrete columns (pillars) on both buildings are linked by means of elegant curves to the beams above them.

Lola's Café at No. 228, encouraged by the deep shade created by the verandah, spills out on the pavement and, with the aid of potted shrubs, adds to the relaxed atmosphere of upper Long Street.

No. 229 Long Street
Cool Runnings Bar

Because the average 'old' building in Long Street has a frontage of 15–20 metres, this two-storey 1930s building lays claim to having the longest verandah – 30 metres! The tiled gabled roof is broken in the centre by a raised section under a hipped roof. The architect created a perfectly symmetrical face for the building with five windows on either side of the central feature – a Venetian window (a composite group of three windows, the middle one under a semi-circular arch).

Although the colour schemes of buildings are transient, for my watercolour I elected to paint the crimson and green over-sized tropical leaves currently decorating the upper wall. The view is taken from across the street from behind the massive Victorian cast-iron columns of the Blue Lodge. By contrast, the railings and supports of the Cool Runnings verandah are not original and were probably part of a recent upgrade.

Above: *No. 229*
Opposite:
No. 226/228

Desmond Martin

No. 230 Long Street

Overseas Visitors' Club and Maharajah Indian Restaurant

The elegant nine-column colonnade that wraps around this three-storey building from Long Street into Buiten Street has a distinct Indian colonial feel, further suggested by the restaurant's name over the splayed corner. The shaded space on street level is repeated on the first floor by another nine columns that support the roof over the verandah with its precast balusters. The top floor and tiled roof were probably added later, possibly in the 1920s.

The ground floor was previously an old-fashioned public bar, 'The Harp'. Take a moment to find the harp motif in leaded glass that still survives in the fanlight above the door on the corner. Small panes in the round-headed windows on street level contribute to the 'old English pub' exterior while the flags of six nations fluttering from the verandah add to the touristy atmosphere of upper Long Street.

Barely visible on the far left in my watercolour is No. 232/234/236 Long Street, a single-storey Victorian shop painted in light tan and cream. It carries a high parapet and a corrugated-iron roof over the pavement, the old columns now replaced with disappointingly plain steel poles. Originally a dwelling, the building was converted into shops in 1900 by the architect John Parker. Though the last of the even-numbered buildings in Long Street, I found it full of surprises: Select Books (No. 232) has innumerable 'scarce, out-of-print and new' books on southern Africa, No. 234 is Detour Travellers Shop, while the other shop, Marvel, is one of the street's vibrant cafés.

Above: *Stained-glass fanlight above the entrance*
Opposite: *No. 230*

No. 251 Long Street *(cnr of Green Street)*
The Dubliner at Kennedy's (formerly the Mountain View Hotel)

Once a dingy 'downtown' hotel, the building now houses the upmarket Dubliner lounge and Kennedy's Irish Restaurant in a striking crimson and buff colour scheme. The original building is a two-storey 1930s construction with a splayed corner and a concrete verandah on six brick piers (pillars) facing Long Street. Note the small faggot bricks used for these piers, each one finished at the top with a simple design. Doric columns support the tiled verandah roof. The original open verandah with its precast balusters and two criss-cross panels was enclosed with timber windows at some later stage. A balustraded parapet neatly finishes the top of the building.

The original hotel entrance was a tall, narrow door set between two small windows (on the far left) in Green Street. Timber columns flank the corner entrance to the refurbished lounge (The Dubliner) on Long Street. You may be able to see the ornate pressed metal ceiling if you venture inside, otherwise enjoy the refreshments at the pavement benches. My watercolour shows one of the few trees in Long Street and, rising like a white spectre behind the restaurant, the outline of Carnival Court, the next building on the street.

Above: *Top of faggot brick pier*
Opposite: *No. 251*

Desmond Martin

No. 255/257/259/261 Long Street

Carnival Court (Carnival Backpackers, Long Street Café, formerly Cranfords Bookshop)

Arguably the centre of the vibrant 'restaurant and bar strip' of Long Street, Carnival Court also has other claims to being the focal point of the area. Architecturally speaking, the building is Victorian fussiness at its best. Its two-storey verandah, cast-iron columns and brackets, and intricate wrought-iron railings form the stage for the symmetry of the third floor and attic rooms with an intricate web of pilasters, swags and cornices that terminate in the two towers and three gables on the skyline. The whole front elevation is dramatically delineated at either end by a tall, decorated chimney. On the ground floor the period shop fronts, expertly crafted in teak, have largely been retained.

Carnival Court was designed in 1901 by the English architect George Ransome. It was built in the following year as luxury apartments for the elite of Cape Town. Over a hundred years later, the accommodation tradition is continued by Carnival Backpackers. I became familiar with the building in 1954 when as a student I shopped for textbooks at the famous Cranfords Bookshop on the ground floor. As the 1985 newspaper advertisement shows, Cranfords had the reputation for having 'the wildest selection of books in the Southern Hemisphere'. Was this meant to read 'the widest selection'? I still have my 1931 edition of Banister Fletcher's *A History of Architecture* that I purchased at Cranfords. Though Cranfords is long gone, Capetonians and its many visitors now relax at the pavement benches or inside tables of the commodious Long Street Café.

Above: *Detail of railing*
Opposite: *No. 255/257/259/261*
Below: *Newspaper advertisement for Cranfords, 1985*

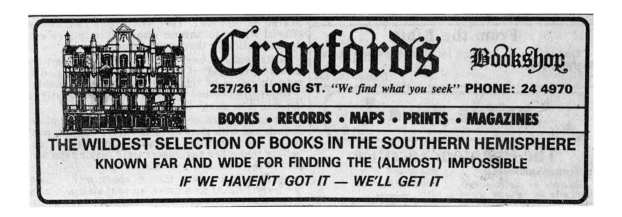

Desmond Martin

No. 263/271 Long Street
Café Mojita, Khaya Nyama, Daddy Longlegs

There is a simple but sad story behind this Long Street veteran: once it sported a cast-iron verandah as attractive as others on the street. Probably as a result of neglect, it deteriorated and was taken down for safety reasons, some time in the 1960s. Immediately below the four double doors you can see the scars in the plaster that indicate the original position of the verandah. Though mutilated through the removal process, this double-storey Victorian building still presents an appealing front as the simple lines of the panelled parapet and cornice can be more easily appreciated. These characteristics are typical of the assertive style of John Parker who designed the building in 1900.

Below each of the two small pediments is a single sash window flanked by the doors that originally led onto the verandah. These doors are now neatly railed off with wrought-iron screens. If you look on the extreme edge of the building on both sides (at head height) you will see the remnant of the cast-iron bracket that supported the 'broekie lace' that decorated the underside of the verandah.

Above: *Cast-iron*
wall bracket
Opposite:
No. 263/271

Desmond Martin

No. 273/275/277 Long Street
Royale Eatery

This eclectic three-storey structure appears to have changed its face several times since it was originally built, possibly in the 1890s. In 1902, AR Wojciechowski added two floors to the existing single-storey building. Rennie noted in 1977 that a canopy or verandah had been removed and suspected that the façade had been rebuilt in the 1940s as suggested by the steel windows. There has been an obvious attempt since 1977 to emphasize existing or introduce new Art Deco elements because the semi-circular centrepiece on the high parapet (with the date '1862') does not show in the survey photograph and no trace remains of the golden brown facebrick noted in the survey. Despite its dubious architectural pedigree I think that the little building with its bright orange and white colour scheme makes an unusual contribution to the streetscape. Don't miss the turned timber joinery over the door of No. 277.

The Royale Eatery is totally committed to the restaurant and bar trade. Their latest innovation is a smart drinks deck built on the narrow roof of the building but cleverly out of sight from the street.

No. 279/283 Long Street
Key Boutique, Nylon Clothing

This simple two-storey building has a quiet dignity unlike its neighbour, the Royale Eatery. Designed by Fred Cherry in 1900, the balustraded parapet, small pedimented gable and Victorian cornice are typical of the era. Its double-storey cast-iron verandah, lost some time during its one hundred-year history, was replaced, possibly in the 1930s, by a corrugated-iron canopy standing on concrete columns. The charm of the ground floor façade is the timber door to No. 281, set between timber pilasters with delicately carved capitals.

Opposite:
Nos. 273/275/277
and 279/283

Desmond Martin

No. 295/297 Long Street *(cnr of Vredenburg Lane)*
Long Street Liquors (formerly Gardens Bottle Store)

Virtually every building in Long Street has something unique about it. In the case of this bottle store it is the only building in the entire length of the street with a distinctive ornate 'wavy' Cape Revival parapet. This feature comprises a series of shallow curves linked together across the top of the building. A circular, louvred window directly below each of the three curves provides ventilation for the shop below. The moulding of the centre curve in the parapet continues onto the face of the parapet with two curves meeting under an anthemion (a stylized decoration used in Greek temples).

Three maroon blinds, invariably drawn to screen the hot afternoon sun from baking the bottled merchandise in the old teak windows, add a touch of colour between the four square pillars standing on the pavement. The heavy concrete and brick verandah supported by these pillars with their square capitals tends to dominate the frontage despite the partial balustrading of the verandah wall. You will need to stand back to see the teak small-pane windows and double doors that open onto the verandah.

Above: *Decorated capital on pillar*
Opposite:
No. 295/297

Desmond Martin

Desmond Martin

No. 301/303 Long Street

Victoria Court

The plan of these flats, built in the 1930s, is like an enormous upside down 'U' or 'hollow square' with the ends of the two arms facing Long Street while the middle section connecting the arms is set well back. A well-executed sandstone wall and pergola with concrete columns screens most of the building and the enclosed garden from the street. All that passers-by see of the three-storey court are the two ends of the 'U', unless you peer, as I did, through the iron gate in the centre. Victoria Court has a colonnaded courtyard reminiscent of the cloisters of ecclesiastical buildings. Rennie comments in his survey that as long ago as the 1850s a two-storey, U-shaped, thick-walled warehouse stood on the site. The present three-storey building incorporates the older two-storey fabric and layout.

My watercolour shows the upper end of Victoria Court where it abuts Cameron Flats. Ladies may want to pop into the Black Lily Ladies Fashions on the ground floor. Two balustraded balconies are supported respectively, on the second floor, by small, cantilevered beams and, on the first floor, by three impressive cantilevered arches that project from the outer walls and columns. Doors opening onto the balconies have semi-circular fanlights above the doors and windows are of the small-paned casement type, typical of the architecture of flats in the pre-World War II era.

No. 305 Long Street

Cat & Moose Backpackers (Cameron Flats)

This is a simple two-storey building with a roofed brick and concrete verandah, standing on four Roman Doric columns, all currently painted in a warm orange. The corrugated roof over the verandah rises to a small pediment in the centre. The teak shop fronts and windows, part of the complete 1930s rebuild of the original building on the site, are still intact.

Opposite:
Nos. 301/303
and 305

Desmond Martin

No. 309/311 Long St

One World Travel Centre

(formerly Garden's Pharmacy and Lennon Ltd)

Looking like an overdressed doll's house, this two-storey Edwardian pharmacy with a dwelling on the first floor was built in 1897 probably to a design by Anthony de Witt (1852-1916) who designed a number of pharmacies for Lennon Limited. Note the steep asbestos slate roof set between stepped gables and the ornamental, balustraded parapet with its two louvred, circular ventilation openings. The focal point of the building is the open pediment in the centre that carries the date '1897' within a decorated panel topped by yet another but smaller open pediment. Hood moulds supported by consoles and pilasters cover the first floor windows.

The concrete and steel joist verandah on four concrete columns also carries a balustrade that matches the parapet balustrading. Up until 1977 the shop featured the name 'LENNON LTD' in large cast-iron letters on the roof ridge. In keeping with the current trend, all the plasterwork is painted white which contrasts well against the dull yellow walls and roof tiles. Inside the shop and above the masses of travel literature on offer is a rare dentilled timber ceiling that you should not miss seeing.

Above: *Louvred ventilation opening decorated with volutes and swag*
Opposite:
No. 309/311

Desmond Martin

Long Street (no number)

Long Street Baths

Just before Long Street becomes Kloof Street, at the end of your long walk up from the Foreshore, are the Long Street Baths. Opened to the public on 4th November 1908, this amenity is still in use despite the passing of nearly 100 years. A commemorative tablet in the entrance hall records that the Mayor of Cape Town at the time, Councillor Fred W Smith inaugurated the baths that were built by the contractor, WJ Parrack. No mention is made on the tablet of the architects, MacGillivray and Grant. Another plaque records that the Turkish Baths, still in operation, were inaugurated on 3 May 1927.

Assuming that you are not intending to swim, all you will see of the baths behind the row of small palms is an unimposing, pale blue, single-storey, plastered building under a flat roof. It has four, rectangular, timber windows in one section fronting the street and, in a shorter section set back two metres, two entrance doors and a window. The most noteworthy architectural feature is the continuous projecting window hood that links all the windows and doors together under a series of shallow curves like the humps on the fictitious Loch Ness monster.

The baths were never an attraction for the YM lads of 1955 as the beaches of the Atlantic Ocean were not too far away. Nevertheless, I did swim once in the baths though I thought the humidity slightly oppressive. On a recent visit, however, I found the enclosed pool well maintained and I think I should have my second swim after all these years. Look for the charming wall poster from the 1900s in the foyer that shows gentlemen, one of whom has two right feet, in long red 'swimming trunks' on the diving board.

Opposite:
Long Street Baths

Desmond Martin

Corner of Long and Buitensingel Streets
St Martini Church (German Lutheran)

Soaring high above the bustle of the intersection of Long, Buitensingel, Kloof and Orange Streets, the steeple (tower and spire) of St Martini's signals the top of Long Street. Designed by Peter Penketh and also built by him between 1851 and 1854, the church is an early example of the Gothic Revival, a style that was extensively used for churches built in Cape Town until well into the 1900s.

The nave with its tall, pointed windows is rather plain; it is the church's impressive steeple that merits more than a casual look. Above the church's main entrance at the base of the square tower is a pentagonal Gothic balcony with delicate pinnacles. Higher up the tower is a triplet lancet (a group of three narrow pointed windows), a feature that is repeated on all four faces. The octagonal spire rises up from the tower behind a parapet of small, pointed, Gothic arches, terminating in a large ornate cross, a 1975 fibreglass replica of the original.

The interior with its decorated roof trusses, fine pulpit and timber reredos, is well worth seeing if you have the time and can obtain permission to view.

Opposite:
St Martini Church

Final thoughts

Without doubt, despite the pressures of property developers, the old fabric of Long Street has improved significantly since 1955, my year at No. 44. Most of the older buildings are treated with respect and many have been recycled and improved without disturbing the original design. With a few exceptions in upper Long Street, the infill architecture has taken into consideration the character of the long-established structures alongside. In a number of restored buildings, old walls have been incorporated into the décor of refurbished premises. Sidewalks in certain parts are being paved with brick and property owners are redecorating their buildings in exciting colour schemes. Sidewalk cafés, coffee bars and restaurants are blossoming and the street continues to be a vibrant artery in the city.

For these and other positive signs to retain the best of the past and to enjoy the finest of the present, Capetonians must be thankful. Provided protective legislation remains in place and all stakeholders in our city continue to recognize the unique contribution Long Street makes to the local economy, its future looks secure and bright; it will remain what Désirée Picton-Seymour in 1977 called, 'Cape Town's most Victorian thoroughfare, both in fact and in spirit'.

Glossary of building and architectural terms

1

ANTHEMION: A stylized ornament in Greek and Roman architecture based on the flower of the honeysuckle.

ARCHITRAVE: A moulding surrounding internal or external openings.

ART DECO: A decorative art style from the 1920s and 1930s, applied to buildings and characterized by stepping lines, planes and geometric shapes such as squares and circles.

ASHLAR: Blocks of stone (masonry) precisely cut and squared and given a smooth finish and laid in regular courses.

BALCONETTE: A small balcony.

BALCONY: A platform projecting from an upstairs door supported on columns or brackets or cantilevers and usually fitted with a rail or wall to provide protection.

BALUSTER: A small pillar or post supporting a handrail or coping.

BALUSTRADE: A series or row of balusters.

'BROEKIE LACE': A local term for delicate decorative cast-ironwork in a railing, derived from the fine lace on ladies' underwear, i.e. (Afrikaans) 'broekie' = pantie.

BROKEN PEDIMENT: A pediment in which the horizontal base mould on which the two sloping members stand is incomplete in the centre.

CASEMENT WINDOW: A window hinged on one side so as to open outwards or inwards.

COLUMN: An upright circular shaft, usually crafted from stone or concrete, designed to support a part of a building such as a beam, balcony or arch.

CONSOLE: An elongated bracket in Greek and Roman architecture in the form of an 'S' and used to support a cornice, windowsill or balcony.

2

CORNICE: A projecting moulding, often ornamented, usually at the top of a building or wall, or trimming a ceiling.

CUPOLA: A small domed roof on top of a tower.

DADO: The lower part of a wall between skirting and chair rail.

DENTILLED: When a cornice or moulding has a series of small square blocks immediately underneath it (resembling a row of teeth), it is said to be 'dentilled'.

DORMER WINDOW: A window projecting from a sloping roof and having its own roof.

EGG-AND-DART: One of the many designs carved on classical ornamental mouldings.

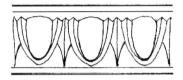

3

ENCAUSTIC TILES: Floor and wall tiles with a decorative design achieved through the use of different coloured clays.

ESCUTCHEON: An ornamented shield, usually in plaster, used for decorating walls (see page 62).

FAGGOT BRICKS: Small bricks used for scale effect typically on column bases and fireplace surrounds.

FESTOON: Refer to the entry opposite for 'SWAG'.

FINIAL: A pointed or rounded ornamentation crowning the top of a pediment, gable or pinnacle.

FRET: A continuous classical pattern of vertical and horizontal lines, often incised into temple walls.

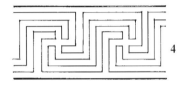

4

GABLE: The triangular upper part of a wall at the end of a building with a pitched roof (end gable); also freestanding above doors and windows, often with curved or pedimented heads.

GABLET: A small gable, sometimes at the top of pillars or buttresses.

HOOD MOULD: A projecting ridge or moulding on a wall above a window, door or arch.

INTERNATIONAL STYLE: An architectural style of the twentieth century characterized by the skyscrapers of most cities. Buildings are generally high-rise, asymmetrical, cubic shapes with minimal decoration and bands of large windows.

ITALIANATE: Relating to the Italian Renaissance, which incorporates Roman motifs.

KEYSTONE: The centre stone or brick in an arch – it holds the 'key' to the arch stability.

LEADED: Windows with small glass panes, often diamond shaped, set in grooved lead bars.

MODILLION: A small classical bracket, used in rows to support a cornice or pediment.

5

MULLION: A vertical bar in a window dividing it in two or smaller sections called 'lights'.

OPEN PEDIMENT: A pediment in which the apex of the triangular shape is missing (see page 52).

ORIEL WINDOW: A bay window projecting from an upper storey of a building and supported on brackets or a curved corbelled wall (see page 49).

PARAPET: A low wall built at the roof edge of a building, house or bridge to prevent persons falling; in Victorian times the parapet wall was more of a decorative feature.

PEDESTAL: The base supporting a column, statue or urn.

PEDIMENT: A low-pitched, triangular extension of a wall, usually at the top and centre of a building. Smaller pediments are used as decorative features above doors and windows.

6

PIER: A freestanding square pillar, usually of brick or concrete, designed to support a part of a building such as a beam, balcony or arch.

PILASTER: A rectangular column projecting slightly from a wall; often decorated.

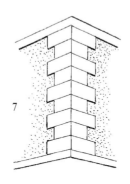

7

QUOINS: The stones at the corner of a building laid alternately, one long face and one short.

RUSTICATED: Stones laid with deep joints between them, usually at the base of a building.

SASH WINDOW: A window consisting of counterbalanced glazed frames that slide up and down in channels in the frame.

STRING COURSE: A projecting course of brick or stone in a wall, often moulded.

SWAG: A decorative ornament in plaster composed of draped material, fixed at two ends and hanging in a curve. If the decoration consists of flowers or foliage, it is termed a 'festoon'.

TERRACOTTA: A hard-burnt, durable facing popular for façades towards the end of the nineteenth century.

TERRAZZO: A wall or floor finish consisting of stone or marble chips set in a tinted cement matrix.

VOLUTE: A decorative device in classical architecture comprising a spiral scroll (see page 56).

VOUSSOIR: A wedge-shaped stone in an arch.

1. Anthemion
2. Console
3. Egg-and-dart moulding
4. Fret
5. Modillion
6. Pediment
7. Quoins

Index